Dateable

Are You? Are They?

Justin Lookadoo

and

Hayley Morgan

Fleming H. Revellation

A Division of Baker Book House Co
Grand Rapids, Michigan 49516

To book Justin and Hayley for speaking engagements,
prevention assemblies for schools, or leadership conferences, or to find out more about Dateable Conferences,
contact them at:

P.O. Box 832 • Mineola, TX 75773
speakers@lookadoo.com

Interior design by Brian Brunsting

Doodles by: Justin, HAYLEY + Brian

Thanks...

Justin: I want to thank Hayley for all the hard work she has put in on this book. Without her I wouldn't have a clue what women want.

Hayley: Aw, that's so sweet, but frankly you still don't have a clue what women want. Hey, you sure sound like you do in this book though. Working with you on this was wonderful and frustrating. Men truly are from Mars.

Justin: This book just goes to show that guys and girls can work together to create something really cool. Man, I hope this book helps other people figure out relationships like it has helped us.

Hayley: Thanks for teaching me about my passions in life and helping me give wings to them. Even though you totally think wrongly sometimes (so like a male), I still have to give you credit for helping me out the door of my fear and into the wide world of my life. Thanks for allowing me to pretend to be you as we wrote this thing. Just promise me I'll never have to do that again.

Justin: I promise. . . . But remember, I'm a guy. I lie to get what I want. Now give me a kiss.

- smack

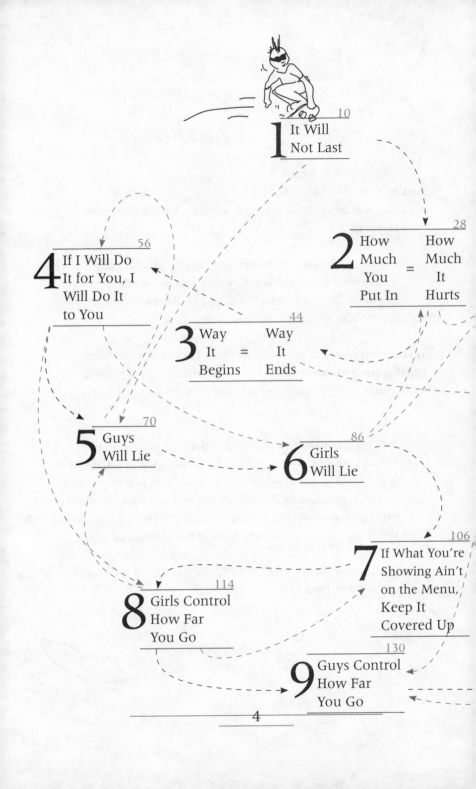

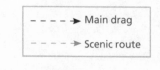

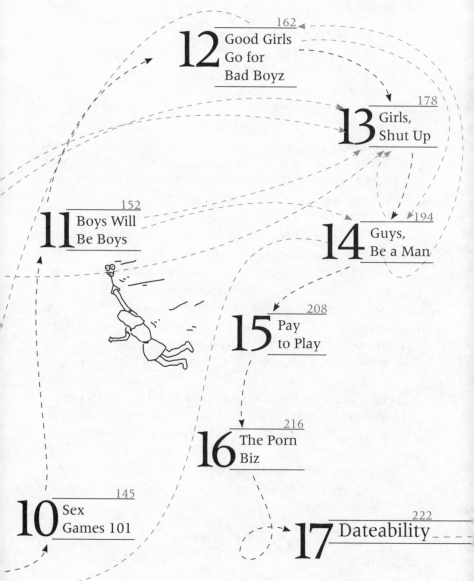

So Who Are Justin and Hayley Anyway?

It takes two to figure out the differences between guys and girls, and we have done it along with the help of "I." Of course, before you get to the "I," we should tell you who we are. Here's the deal with us.

Justin Lookadoo is an award-winning juvenile probation officer who really understands the way guys think and act. He spent over 5 years working with teens living in the danger zone and now spends all his time speaking to the masses in public high schools and at leadership camps like MADD, DARE, and others. That makes 10 years of hanging out with teenagers! He has spoken to over 350,000 students and has been labeled "the speaker and author for the ADD generation." Young people don't have the focus of previous generations and neither does Justin, so as he bounces from point to point, audiences and readers have to keep the pace and enjoy the ride. It will never be boring. Justin doesn't believe in beating around the bush. He gets straight to the point and tells you exactly how it is, even if it isn't so pretty. Justin is also the author of *Step Off: The Hardest 30 Days of Your Life* and coauthor of *Extreme Encounters* and *Ask Hayley/Ask Justin*.

Is my nose too big?

Hayley Morgan is the sensible voice in the mix. She is a former process manager for Nike, Inc., and more recently developer and brand manager of Extreme for Jesus, a line of teen books and Bibles published by Thomas Nelson Publishers. She has developed over 30 titles for teens, including *Ask Hayley/Ask Justin* and *Extreme Encounters*. She now speaks to teens and teaches others how to create and develop products that connect with the ADD minds of America. When you come across the kind, inspirational words in this book, you will know they came from Hayley. Her job was to add the encouragement and hope in this quest to become *Dateable*.

"I" is the combination of the minds of Hayley and Justin. For this book the "we" became "I" so that you don't have to figure out who the heck is talking. Enjoy Justin's voice—he plays "I" in this book—but listen carefully and you'll begin to hear the sensitive side. Then you'll know you found the Hayley in "I."

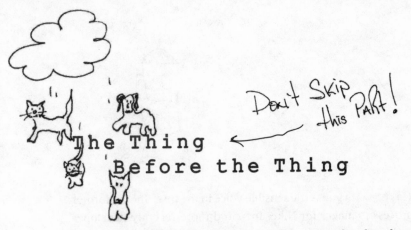

Don't Skip this Part!

The Thing Before the Thing

This book is all about being *Dateable*. The how, the why, the when, the whole package. But before we get to that, we have to start at the beginning—with the passion. Passion isn't just a sexual thing. It's much bigger than that. Passion is your life. What you do and how you do it. It's what pushes you and makes you successful. It's what drives people to fight for freedom, to give their lives for others, and to search for the cure for cancer. It's what makes warriors strong and princesses desirable. It's what makes your dreams a reality. Passion in the hands of a wise man or woman is the key to unlocking destiny, but passion abused is destruction, pain, and heartache.

Passion is fuel. When contained and used properly, it's the fuel that propels unimaginable feats. It propels a jet plane. It gets people to the moon. But that same passion, when used carelessly or for selfish endeavors, is explosive. It can destroy you and everybody around you. The desires you have deep inside you can propel you to greatness or destroy your life in a single spark. If you can't control your passion, you can't control your future. So being *Dateable* is not about hooking up, it's about exposing your passion and discovering your destiny. A lot of what you'll read in these pages you're not going to like. But it's not about you, it's about how passion can become destructive and the power you have to redirect it for a greater pur-

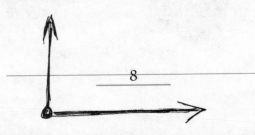

8

pose. So push through the hard parts and let it sink in so it can ignite the passion within you that will change the world. What's your passion in life? What gets you totally cranked up? Each of us has been given a passion. The Creator has wired us with a burning desire deep within us. It has nothing to do with relationships. There is something we want to do—no, that we *have* to do. It could be teaching. It could be painting, writing, or building. It's different for everyone, but the desire is the same and it won't be ignored.

But so often we focus our energy and our desire on *someone* else. A person. A crush. We never get to explore that destiny we were designed for because we're so busy trying to get someone to like us. We put our lives on hold because we think we will automatically accomplish all the great stuff when we get old. But the only reason we have to wait 'til we get old is that we're too busy chasing hotties in high school. I have no doubt that most revolutionary things could have been done earlier if the people called to do them hadn't been messing around for so long. Just think about it. Get out a piece of paper right now and write down everything you would love to do. Make it big stuff: write a book, find the cure for cancer, backpack across Europe, swim with dolphins, restore an old hot rod, play college ball. Write down all the stuff you want to do in life.

Now look at your list. You *can* do these things. I'm not saying it won't take a little effort—it will. But with energy behind your passion and focus behind your mission, you can begin to accomplish the things on your list today. Don't let your plans get distracted by the search for love. Dream big dreams and trust the Planner of the universe to bring you your big love. You have a mission. If you choose to accept it, you will soar with eagles. You will walk and not grow weary. You will run and not faint. *That* will last! The relationship won't.

1

It

Will

Not

Last

Screech! *What did he just say?*

You heard me. Whatever relationship you are in right now, whether you are 14, 15, 16, or even 18 years old, know this: *It will not last!* Period. The end. I know, you are sixteen and *sooo* into this guy or girl—but understand that this relationship will not last. You will break up. It will end. It will hurt. It will get in the way of your purpose in life, and it will complicate things and distract you from your passion and destiny.

I know, I know. I'm wrong about *your* relationship. It's different. You're the exception. You're right for each other. You can just feel it. You have so much in common. You like the same movies. You know each other so deeply that you even finish each other's sentences. You know what the other is thinking. It hurts when you're apart. Congrats! But that has nothing to do with it.

Hang with me now. I know it's a bummer to think about and even harder to accept. You may even refuse to accept it. But that doesn't change the fact that it's true. I may believe I don't have to wear clothes to school, but that doesn't mean I'm right. Just because you *believe* your relationship is different doesn't mean it is.

I'm not trying to throw a Valium in the middle of the upper moment you have going with your bf or gf, but you have to accept this fact. If you don't, dating will destroy you. It will rip you apart piece by piece. Crush by crush. But when (and only

when) you accept the fact that it will not last, you can totally enjoy this dating thing.

For those of you who are die-hard romantics who have bought into Hollywood's version of Romeo-and-Juliet-teen-love-at-first-sight (movies which are usually played by actors who are on their third or fourth marriages, by the way), let's play it this way. Check these facts: Out of 100 married people asked, 22 said that they married their high school crush. Sounds great, huh? Maybe there is hope. But check this: Out of those 22 people, 17 got divorced. So 5 out of 100 people between the ages of 18 and 89 are still married to their high school sweethearts. Ouch! So you and your crush have two options—one, get married; two, break up. That's it. Get married or break up. The percentages speak for themselves. Still not convinced? Try this.

The average age people get married is 25. So take 25 and subtract your age. We'll call your answer "years left" (see formula

below). That's how many years you have left, on average, before you marry. Now, write down how many crushes you have had in the last 12 months. Got it? Now take the number of crushes and multiply it by your "years left." The number you get is the number of crushes you will have before you get married.

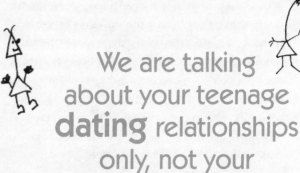

$$25 - \underline{}_{\text{your age}} = \underline{}_{\text{years left}}$$

$$\underline{}_{\substack{\text{number of crushes} \\ \text{in last 12 months}}} \times \underline{}_{\text{years left}} = \underline{}_{\substack{\text{number of crushes} \\ \text{'til you find} \\ \text{"the one"}}}$$

Now if you're one of those hardheads who thinks, "I'll show him. We *are* different. It's gonna work!" don't do something stupid like run out and get married and then call me to say, "See, I told you we were meant for each other." No! Don't call me

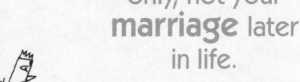

We are talking about your teenage **dating** relationships only, not your **marriage** later in life.

after 2 years, or after 5, 10, or even 20 years. Give me a call after you've been married 35 years. Then you can say I was wrong about *your* relationship. You'll be about 52 years old. Call me and scream as loud as you can, "I told you so!" I won't hold my breath, though. See, *getting* married is not the issue. Anyone can do that. It's *staying* married that is the goal.

Here's why it's so important to accept that it will not last: If you hold onto the hope that *your* relationship will last and that *you* will defy all the odds, then you give away too much and waste your teen dating years. You end up so zoned on trying to make it work that you miss out on the best parts of the experience of dating. You set yourself up for failure. I want you to succeed. With the truth in this book, you'll know how to protect your heart and live with excitement and passion. I'm not knocking the dating process. I think it can be fun if you have the right goals in mind. I just don't want you to put so much pressure on the relationship that you take all the fun out of it. I want you to date, but even more, I want you to be *Dateable.*

Let's break it down and check some of the hardcore issues. First, let me tell you where I'm starting from. You need to understand some solid truths. Let's start with some basic things we can agree on:

> **TRUTH:** Just because you date someone doesn't mean you will marry them.
>
> **TRUTH:** Your dating experience will help shape your married life.

TRUTH: You will date several people before you get married.

TRUTH: Your spiritual beliefs have an impact on your dating life.

We can all agree on these truths. This is our baseline. Now let's look at what accepting "it will not last" as a truth will do for you.

Totally accepting that the relationship will not last does not cheapen it or make it less important. In reality, it makes the relationship *more* valuable. You know that you only have it for a short time, so it becomes more important to you. You want to savor it more. You appreciate it more. You learn from it and protect it. If you truly understand that the relationship has an end, then the sweet little things will become important and the giant ugly things—like how he didn't call—will become no biggies. Would you rather waste your time freaking out about everything or enjoy the time you have? You know it won't last forever, so yeah, you want to enjoy it while you can.

Also, when you **accept the truth**, the pressure's off. A lot of lives are destroyed because of pressure to make a dating relationship work. If you believe that the relationship is meant to be, then you will do stupid things to keep it going. That's where couples can really mess up. You can get into a cycle that you just can't seem to get out of. You might get into sex to make the other person happy. You might try manipulation, violence, or using each other. You worry that your friends won't understand or won't like you if you break up. Or worse yet, your parents might get upset if you break up with "the perfect person." That's just not cool. Don't let others force you into a relationship that isn't right.

Let me throw in a commercial here. *Do not get your family deeply involved in your relationships.* Let me repeat that: Do not get your family deeply involved.

Sure, you need to let them know who your friends are and who you are dating, but **don't allow your dating life to get too tight with your family life**. I mean, it's one thing to spend time with your bf/gf at home or hanging out with your family. That's not horrible, but it's a totally different issue to let your bf/gf get so involved in your family that they are as much of a fixture as you are. They're not your significant other. And no one becomes part of your family until you marry them. **Making them part of the fam is way too much pressure.** And what's worse is that it can make you get stuck in a relationship you want to get out of, because you not only have to break up with your crush, but you have to break up with the entire family. It's just not healthy.

You don't have to worry about any of this if you start the relationship already knowing it will eventually end. You can relax. The end might come this week or it might come eight months from now. It's okay. Just part of the deal. And you won't have to compromise who you are or what you believe just to feel accepted. If your boyfriend really wants you to have sex, you don't have to give in to try to keep him. Why would you?

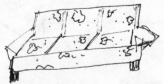

So it will last another week? Hey, you can just consider this the end of the relationship. No big deal. You knew it was coming. Yeah, there will still be some pain, but nothing like there could have been (more on that in *How Much You Put In Determines How Much It Will Hurt When It Ends*). You are protected from a lot of pain because you understand that it isn't going to last anyway.

Now let's look at this from the spiritual side. God knows that if we get too caught up in chasing, catching, and hanging onto a crush, then we stop growing. We stop seeing his power. His mystery. His love. The Great Romancer wants to romance you. He wants to show you the sunsets and give you the falling stars. He wants you to run with passion after him. He wants to shape you. He wants to give you your dreams, your desires, your destiny. But he can't do that if your crush already has your total focus.

Dating is supposed to be fun. It's supposed to be safe. But we invest way too much in trying to make it work out. If we just let go and understand that it's a short-term thing, then we get the most out of it. We learn about ourselves. We learn about others. We experience a crazy, fun part of life, and we don't get destroyed during the process. We end up stronger, happier, and more successful. We understand what makes us tick. What we like. What we don't like. We find that desire that God has placed in us. And we don't get chained to a dying relationship.

NOTE: So far I've been talking mostly to the girls. You know why? 'Cause guys *do not* think it's going to last, as in married, forever, amen. Sure, he may tell you that you will be together

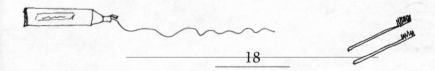

and ever

~~forever.~~ And it *will* seem like forever to him. But teen boys don't think much about things down the road, like planning weddings—that's kind of a girl obsession. A guy's forever is more short-term than a girl's forever.

So, girls, while you are planning *your* life together, he's thinking about *his* future. He's thinking about what he wants to do with *his* life. Not *your* married life together! Marriage is not really a factor to him. Even if you decide to go to the same college to be with each other, *you* are still not the biggest issue in his life. And no, asking him if this is true will *not* clear things up. He will tell you what you want to hear, not the truth (see *Guys Will Lie to You to Get What They Want*).

All this doesn't mean guys are jerks and girls are great. It just means that we all have different ways of looking at things. The balance of the universe depends on this. Girls are home-builders—you create, you give birth, you nurture and protect your families. So you tend to be on the lookout for the perfect home, the perfect provider, the perfect husband. It's the way you're wired. Guys are hunters—they have to go off to conquer and

> No matter how much you talk about the future, guys do not believe you will be together forever—he's not thinking about marriage.

Ch. 5

What Should a Guy Say?

Nothing

My first suggestion for guys is to **tell the truth**: "I'm so glad we are together *right now*." Problem is, what will a girl believe you mean? "He knows we're meant to be together. He feels the same way I do. He's the one."

So what about **the brutal truth?** "I'm glad we are dating now because this will make me a better man for my future wife." That's the truth, but what happens when you say it? Smack! It just doesn't fly.

Here's the problem: No matter what guys say, **girls tend to attach strings**. So guys, I can't help you much other than to say be careful with your words. Tell them honestly how you feel, and don't exaggerate.

Ooohh, huh?.

save the world. It's the way they were designed. So it isn't being horrible jerks that makes them this way; it's a well-designed plan. Once we all figure that out and are cool with it, we can start to have healthy relationships.

Now guys, you need to understand where the girls are coming from on this. They really think you are going to be together for the next 10 to 20 years, maybe even the rest of your life. As soon as a girl starts crushing on a guy, this whole dream world kicks into motion. She produces and directs this movie in her mind about the two of you. She sees the two of you laughing and playing together and you totally digging her. She is already picking out names for your kids.

Guys, hear me now, believe me later: The girl who has a crush on you is practicing signing her first name with your last name! Don't think she's not. She is! She starts that before you even start dating for real. She talks with her friends about all of this. They tell her how good you look together and they talk about what your kids will look like. This is even *before* you are officially going out. Don't laugh this off, guys. It's for real.

You need to understand this, fellas, because we are the ones who make the problem worse. It's like this. A girl starts liking us, and then we start telling her what she wants to hear:

"You are the most wonderful girl I've ever met."

"I feel so different when I'm with you."

"I've never met anyone like you."

"I want to be with you forever."

Mrs. Lookadoo   Mrs. Mary Sue Lookadoo   Mrs. Mary Lookadoo   ML   ML   Mrs. MS. Lookadoo

The catch is, guys know they aren't planning a marriage. If someone would push us to think about what we're actually saying, we would know instantly that we *don't mean it like that*. Notice that I didn't say we don't mean it. We just don't mean it *like that*. We know that any hot girl will make us feel different when we are with her. We know this—but girls don't. They think our words are the honest, how-we-feel truth. Girls build their lives and dreams around these words. But for guys, they are just words that we hope will get the girl to like us.

So, guys, help! We are responsible here. Think about what you're saying. You really know that it won't last, so don't pretend. What you are doing is emotional abuse. See, sexual abuse is sex by force or manipulation, and emotional abuse is manipulation of emotions, playing with her feelings. Don't manipulate a girl by purposely saying things that she will misunderstand. Guys, you know that a girl who is crushing on you is going to hang on every word you say. She is going to build a fantasy romance, leaving her vulnerable and willing to do whatever she can to make it work with you. So you take the pureness inside of her, expose it, twist it, and force yourself between her imagination and her dreams. Then you rip it out, use it, destroy it, and leave her to pick up the shattered pieces. All the while, you knew you didn't believe all the stuff you said. You just said it.

STOP! Don't tell her you love her. Don't tell her you want to be with her forever. It's not cool, even if that's what you think right now. Because you're abusing her emotionally if you do. As men, we have been given a responsibility. Take it and be a man.

The guy is in charge of the relationship. You can't let it get blown out of proportion into this "forever-and-ever" thing. Be careful with her heart. Protect it like a mighty warrior. Don't let anyone damage it, not even you. You are the protector.

Some guys who are reading this are saying, "That's not me! I think it's gonna last 'cause I love her. The way I feel is amazing. She *is* the one." Okay, I'll give you that. You do *feel* like it will last forever, so let's talk about that feeling. You can't eat, you can't sleep, you get butterflies in her presence, your palms sweat. You feel like a total dork and it feels great. Newsflash for you: This isn't love. It's somebody else besides your mother thinking you are cool. And it's an amazing feeling. Don't get me wrong, I dig it just as much as you do. But don't confuse the *feeling* with love. Love doesn't feel all mushy. Love isn't sweaty palms and sleepless nights. Love is a decision you make to care for someone no matter how you feel. If they are disfigured in an accident or throwing up for hours on end, you will still love them.

This is **way important** to understand because I want you to cherish your relationship for what it is—an amazing sign that you are accepted. Your relationship means you are special. You know that because someone who doesn't have to care about you does. Let's not bash that. It's part of what gives you confidence and makes life exciting. But it isn't love. Have fun knowing you are lovable. Enjoy the acceptance of a non-family member, but remember, it's not love yet. It's just a great feeling that you can enjoy for now.

The question becomes: Will it *ever* last? Yes! Don't worry. You will find someone that God has designed for you. You will find that soul connection you desire. Right now we're just talking about your teen dating years. The rules totally change later on in life when marriage stuff comes into play. But until then, remember that it will not last.

I hope you can see that by believing the truth "It will not last" you are not being exiled to a wasteland of the un*Dateable*. Actually, it frees you to experience unimaginable excitement and control and sets you on track to being intensely *Dateable*.

Dateable Delusions: Which Stage Are You In?

Stage A. In a relationship.

You are **working hard to keep the love alive**. Beware—you are in danger of compromising and selling out to try to make something last that never had a chance.

Stage 2. Trying to get a relationship.

Work, work, work. You are spending way too much time *trying* to get noticed. Dress, talk, party invites, anything to become a crush magnet. Spending all your energy trying to get someone who will eventually leave you.

Stage π. Wanting a relationship.

Wake up! You **daydream about the fairytale relationship**. You think about how wonderful it would be if only you had one. You are living in a fantasy world instead of experiencing the excitement of real life.

Quiz Time

Will Your Crush Last?

Fill in the blank or circle your answer for each question.

1. You have been dating _____ months.

2. On a scale of one to ten (with ten being the highest), your love is a _____.

3. You plan on getting married at the end of high school.   yes   no

4. You have said "I love you."   yes   no

5. You are sure God told you that your crush is the one.   yes   no

6. You are going to only be friends until you are old enough to marry.   yes   no

7. You can't live without each other.   yes   no

8. You have gone to which base?
   1st   2nd   3rd   4th (home)

Score your answers.

1. Number of months: _____
2. Love rating: _____
3. Yes = 2 points; no = 1 point _____
4. Yes = 2 points; no = 1 point;
   both of you have said it = 3 points _____
5. No = 2 points; yes = 1 point _____
6. No = 2 points; yes = 1 point _____
7. Yes = 2 points; no = 1 point _____
8. Number of bases you have gone to: _____

Add up all the numbers you have written down. What's your score?

20+: **Stop, drop, and roll!** *Your relationship is on fire, and not in a good way. You are on a crash course with tears and pain. I know you don't think so, but believe me, it's true. If you aren't old enough to get a job, pay your own bills, and make a home, then slow the boat down. You're wasting your energy playing house. Read on. This book is for you.*

15-19: *Here's the deal.* **You are doing a good job**—*kinda. But it looks like you are a little too loopy for each other. Slow down! It's not a race. And how fast it starts is how fast it will end (check out* The Way It Begins Is the Way It Will End*). Take time to be friends. It won't kill the relationship if it's what God wants.*

7-14: *Wow!* **Your romance might just have a chance**—*a chance somewhere in the distant future. It looks like you are saving yourself for marriage. Good decision. Hang out. Be friends and wait 'til you are closer to the whole marriage thing before you start dumping everything into a relationship.*

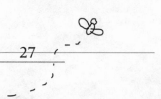

How Much You Put In

Determines How Much
It Will Hurt
When it Ends!

Quiz Time *again*

Heartbreak Hotel

Choose the one that is most true about you and your love:

1. My bf (gf) and I:
   a. talk on the phone a few times a week.
   b. talk on the phone at least an hour a day.
   c. have too much to do to be on the phone all the time.

2. When it comes to spending money:
   a. the sky's the limit for my baby; I spend, spend, spend.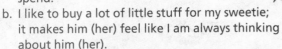
   b. I like to buy a lot of little stuff for my sweetie; it makes him (her) feel like I am always thinking about him (her).
   c. Spend? I'm a student. How can I spend money on someone? I'm broke!

3. Our physical life:
   a. It's amazing—we are exploring all the possibilities of love.
   b. We fool around a little, but we are saving intercourse for our wedding night.
   c. Purity is it, baby! We don't fool around with fooling around. We are too young to be makin' babies.

4. This is how well I know my love:
    a. We try to share the really important stuff with each other so we can get closer.
    b. We tell each other everything! If we are meant to be together, we can't have any secrets.
    c. There are still a lot of things we don't know about each other and that's okay.

5. When people talk about us, they probably say:
    a. "Those two are perfect for each other; it's like they are already married."
    b. "They are both really good kids with great futures."
    c. "They make a cute couple. I hope they'll be together for a long time."

6. Beyond a shadow of a doubt, we are:
    a. madly, 100%, forever in love.
    b. really crazy over each other.
    c. living life one day at a time.

7. On a scale of one to ten (ten being the highest), I would say that this relationship is a:
    a. 5.
    b. 11.
    c. 10.

Now go back and add up your score using the following key:

1. A = 2; B = 3; C = 1 _____
2. A = 3; B = 2; C = 1 _____
3. A = 3; B = 2; C = 1 _____
4. A = 2; B = 3; C = 1 _____
5. A = 3; B = 1; C = 2 _____
6. A = 3; B = 2; C = 1 _____
7. A = 1; B = 3; C = 2 _____

17–21: **Heartbreak Hotel**. *You've just checked in. You are spending way too much of yourself on this crush that won't last. Sorry, I know you think it will, but statistics show that it won't. Now that you've put so much in, expect the pain to be immense when you break up. The breakup will be as powerful as the love is right now, so take cover. You're in for heartache.*

12–16: **Beware**. *You are treading on thin ice. You aren't in danger just yet, but it could be around the corner. Don't lose the mystery. Everyone loves a chase, so slow down and let the friendship grow. Don't give too much or the pain of the breakup will kill.*

7–11: **Well done**. *You have a good head on your shoulders. It's gonna hurt when you break up, but you will recover quickly. Keep on having fun and getting to know each other, but no playing house. You guys are keeping it real.*

ouch

Okay. We agree that the relationship will not last. So let's look at the next thing you need to understand before you can be truly *Dateable*—How much you put into a relationship will determine how much it hurts when it ends.

If you invest everything you have—emotionally, physically, socially, spiritually—in a relationship, you wind up totally destroyed when it ends. <u>You dump your entire existence into a crush,</u> and when it tears you apart you cry out to God, "Why did you let this happen?"

Listen, don't go blamin' God for what *you've* done. All that pain is the result of *you* pouring too much of yourself into a relationship that was *not* going to last in the first place.

Let's get real and break it down so we can see things clearly. Check this out.

Socially Unacceptable

If you arrange your entire social calendar around this person, it will be mammoth pain when it ends. And it won't really have anything to do with the person. See, when you spend every moment with your bf/gf—you wait for each other between classes, eat lunch together, spend every night talking on the phone and the weekends hanging out together—what happens? You totally ditch your friends. You don't mean to, but that's the way it works.

You know this is true. You get in a relationship and are all into this guy. He becomes more and more important to you.

What you don't realize is that the more important he becomes, the less important everyone else becomes. Your friends are the ones who encouraged you to go for it, but now they are the ones you're too busy for. You don't even really notice how little you talk with them. But they notice.

Has that ever happened to you? Your bud just fades into some guy and you feel totally dumped. You feel like you're being left behind. It's not true, but that's how it feels. You don't get the calls or the invites anymore. And when you finally get some "talk time," it's just the same tired rerun about her and her boyfriend.

Fellas, you know you do this too. You know that when you get so hooked on some girl you ditch your friends. Not intentionally, but it happens the same way it happens with girls, only guys have a name for it. It's called *whipped!*

You've seen it happen. If you connect everything you do socially with your crush, then know that it's a major KO when it ends. Not only do you feel hurt because of the breakup, but the pain of the breakup is intensified because you don't have anything to do. You've created a *friend void* and now there's nothing to fill your time. You have no friends to help you through the breakup or just to do stuff with. You're alone to deal with the issues. And what makes it even worse is that when you do get back in the social swing of things and start going solo, everyone comes up and asks, "Where's Chase?" and once again you have to explain how you broke up.

All of this is taken care of when you understand that the relationship will not last. When you know this, you have total control over your life. You can spend time with your crush *and* stay connected to your friends. You can protect those relationships. You'll hang out with your pals on the weekend. You'll have time to chat with them during the week and hang out with them during lunch. You'll be able to keep your friends because you know that your crush is short-lived but your buds are for life. Your entire social life is under your control, and you're in the position of social power.

Physically Fit

The more you pour into a dating relationship physically, the more it will rip you apart when it ends. And different people give in physically for different reasons: To feel accepted. To keep the relationship going. To feel connected. To please themselves or the other person. But the further you go, the more it will hurt. Kissing. Touching. Foreplay. Sex. If you push it sexually, it will destroy you emotionally.

Sex creates a soul connection. It doesn't matter if you want it to or not. God created it that way. So the more you give up sexu- ~~HHL~~ ally in a relationship, the more it rips your soul apart. It creates scars that will never go away. Plus, you become a number.

A lot of people, especially girls, compromise with the sex stuff because they want to feel special and to feel like the relationship is something special. But what you thought made you special

I'm in control!! :)

Just say "No".

How will I feel when he is doing this with my

friend?

to the other person—sex—makes you just like the next girl. There's nothing different about you. Sex doesn't make him want to come back. It's the chase he wants (see *Girls, Shut Up and Be Mysterious*). He can get *sex* from any weak and needy girl that's crushin' on him. And girls, in about seven years, he probably won't even remember your name.

Ch. 13

You know the relationship will end. You will move on and so will he. So before you give in and compromise sexually in any way, ask yourself this: "How will I feel when he's doing this with my friend?" That's right. Whatever you are doing with your bf, he will be doing with someone else. And even worse, ask yourself how you're going to feel when he's doing this with that girl you can't stand. That's right, 'cause where he left off physically with you, he'll pick up physically with the next girl. Holding hands. Kissing. Touching. Sex. Whatever you are doing together, he's also going to do with someone else. So when it's getting all hot and heavy and the passion is just about to explode, just think about how you're going to feel when you are being compared to the next girl. 'Cause you will.

Know that if you give a lot physically in the relationship you will feel stupid, used, dirty, and alone. There's nothing you can do to stop those feelings after it has happened. The only way to come out of the relationship feeling proud and strong is to not give in. Don't compromise. Stay physically fit.

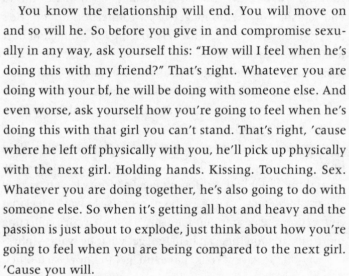

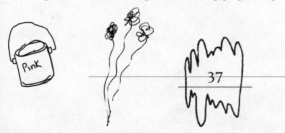

Emotional Wreck

Emotionally, the same rules apply. You get so into this guy and you tell him all your deepest, most personal secrets. What's that going to do to you when it ends? First of all, it's going to hurt a lot more because the emotional tie seems a lot deeper. And think about this: You have told all your intimate stuff to your crush. Now he no longer has a connection to you. He's not committed to you and the relationship left a bunch of hurt feelings. Now what? Not only are you hurt because your emotional roots have been ripped out, but you have a loaded gun running around who could shoot off your most personal stories to anyone. That's an emotional disaster that would destroy you more than the breakup.

What can you do to protect yourself? Save the info. Hold on to your personal details. Your crush doesn't need to know everything about you. He doesn't need a history lesson with all the graphic details. A girl uses this info swap as a way to feel that connection she desires, but for a guy it's strategy. It's collecting more information that can help him get what he wants—physical pay-off. So save it. Talk, have fun, get to know each other. You can share stuff. Just hold back the important, personal stuff. A good guideline is that it should take you two years to unpack your emotional baggage. So pace yourself. After a year of going out, you can start giving up more personal stuff. After two years, you can get deeper. Are you thinking, "I can't wait that long, 'cuz it won't last"? EXACTLY! Save yourself the pain of being too glued together emotionally. Keep your fear factor of blabbed info low and up your *Dateability* by remaining a woman that is mysterious.

Financial Failure

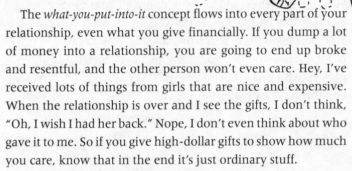

The *what-you-put-into-it* concept flows into every part of your relationship, even what you give financially. If you dump a lot of money into a relationship, you are going to end up broke and resentful, and the other person won't even care. Hey, I've received lots of things from girls that are nice and expensive. When the relationship is over and I see the gifts, I don't think, "Oh, I wish I had her back." Nope, I don't even think about who gave it to me. So if you give high-dollar gifts to show how much you care, know that in the end it's just ordinary stuff.

You may feel like your crush really likes you and appreciates you even more when you start throwing gifts her way. But she doesn't like *you* more, she like the prizes. You run a major danger of becoming the sugar daddy or the money honey. Paying for big-time fun and gifts may make the relationship last longer, but only because your crush wants to keep the good times rollin'.

How much you put into a relationship will determine how much it hurts when it ends. Before we move on, remember that we are talking about dating relationships in your prime teen years. Once you are ready for marriage, the rules change. You have to pour everything into it. Financially, emotionally, physically, spiritually, and socially, everything has to be given to the relationship. But for now we are focusing on how to have fun, live, grow, and experience life as a teenager without getting ripped apart.

Would you put all your money, everything you had, into a jar knowing that someone was going to come by and take it away from you? If you knew that in three weeks the jar would be gone forever, would you still dump all your money into it? Not just "no" but N double O! Well, that's what you do when you pour everything into a relationship. You know that it will be taken from you, but you still pour all of yourself into another person, who gets up, walks away, takes all you have invested, and throws it away like yesterday's garbage.

Commitment-o-Phobia

Now here's where everything gets more confusing. You pour everything into a relationship. You give everything physically, emotionally, socially, financially. You give 'til you have nothing else to give and you call it dating. That is not dating. That is a marriage.

You do this over and over. You get in a relationship that takes all of you. You try to connect so deeply, and then you break up. You give everything and then break up again. You think you're preparing or even practicing for marriage. Wrongsville. *What you are practicing is divorce.* Giving everything and then breaking it off is what happens when a marriage breaks up. Couples have given themselves. They've tried to please the other

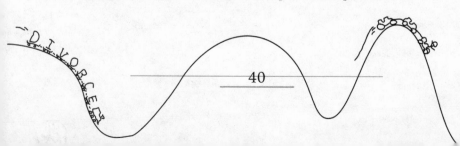

40

playing house with each other.

person. They've done everything to make it work. Their lives were totally entwined and then ripped apart. That's not dating. That's divorce.

When you date, break up, date, break up, understand that you are training your mind that this is how a relationship is supposed to work. You get really close and then you break up. Your mind is conditioned to think that this is what happens in a normal relationship. Just like with anything else, your mind connects the dots when things happen over and over.

Fast forward and watch how this date-and-break-up repetition affects your life. You finally find a guy that you really like. You are at the point where you are ready for marriage and all the stuff that goes with it. Without even knowing it, you will start sabotaging the relationship. You will start seeing problems that aren't really there or overanalyzing stupid little things like how he chews his food weird. You'll get irritated with him and find reasons why the relationship will not work.

Why does this happen? Because your mind has been trained through repetition that this is how a normal relationship works. You get really close to someone, so the next step is to break up. If you don't break up, then something just doesn't feel right. Your mind knows how relationships are supposed to work, and you are supposed to break up now. You will do this even though you don't want to. That's what happens after years of dating and breaking up. It's a bad cycle to get into. It makes divorce easier. So don't practice divorce by playing house with

Practice makes perfect

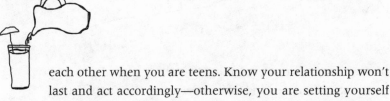

each other when you are teens. Know your relationship won't last and act accordingly—otherwise, you are setting yourself up for disaster.

The more you compromise, pour in, and break up, the more baggage you carry with you. Sexually, emotionally, and mentally, the more you give to the relationship, the more scarred you will get and the more issues you will have to work through later on. Some adults have not been able to enjoy their lives because they could never work through all the issues they created during their teen dating years.

This may sound horrible, but it's not. Have you heard the saying "the truth shall set you free"? That is what all this stuff is about. I'm not filling you in on the truth to freak you out, but to help you stay free. When you understand that what you put in determines the pain when it ends, you become powerful. You are in control of what you do and how much you hurt. You will become happier, more confident, and way more *Dateable*.

So here's the deal. You can assume I'm right, or you can assume I'm wrong. You don't have any other options. You don't really know for sure. If you assume I'm right on this stuff and it turns out I'm wrong about you, what happens? Worst case scenario, you take it slow, you don't compromise, and blam! you end up with a great relationship. You're powerful, you're happy, and 35 years from now you can talk about how wrong I was.

But if you assume I'm wrong and I really am right, what happens? Your heart is shredded. You are scarred. Part of your soul

is ripped out. You have to go through the pain and depression of knowing that you were stupid and could have stopped it.

So what's your choice? If you choose to believe me, you'll be protected and powerful. If you choose to ignore me, don't whine and cry when you are crushed. Every consequence is the result of a choice. What you choose to believe will determine the condition of your heart.

I don't say this to be mean. I say this because I want you to know the truth. I want you to see how valuable you are and to take control of your own happiness and pain. Controlling what you put into a relationship will make you more confident, more secure, and more *Dateable*.

The Way It

Begins

Is the Way

It Will

End

This is the whole law of physics thing. You know, like, "what goes up must come down," or "for every action there is an opposite and equal reaction." The way a relationship begins is the way it will end. See? It fits. It's an equal and opposite reaction.

The *Fast* and Furious Relationship

This kind of relationship is all flame and passion from the beginning. The intensity is so hot you can't resist it. It goes a little like this: You are at a friend's house. You meet this guy and you hit it off. You are all over each other. The music is pumpin' and the people are jumpin' and the two of you just latch on to each other. It's intense. The next week you spend every moment either together or on the phone. It's quick. It's strong. You know immediately that you were supposed to meet and be together.

That's the way it begins, so how will it end?

Fast forward to sometime in the near future. The intensity of passion and fire you felt at the beginning is the same intensity of pain you will feel at the end. The end will be just like the beginning—quick, unexpected, and intense—only painful.

The S l o w Burn Relationship

This relationship is slow and sweet. You start going out with a girl that you have been friends with since first grade. You know

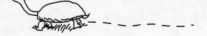

each other. You played together when you were kids. You're friends with her family and she's friends with yours. Now you've gotten closer and you decide to date. Meanwhile, you remember the truths of *it will not last* and *how much you put in determines how much it will hurt when it ends.*

Well, if you have been friends your whole life, when it ends you will probably be nicer to each other than the two who started fast and furious. You will care about each other's feelings because you have been solid friends for so long. Yeah, it will hurt, but the pain may be less intense (but longer lasting) than with those fast, passionate relationships. Why? Because that's what the relationship was. You got to the dating zone with a less intense, long-term relationship that just kept building. Your biggest source of pain will be the damage to the friendship. The bummer is that there is no way you can go back to the way it was. It doesn't matter how much you promise each other or how sincere you are. You cannot go back to "just friends" like before. So that part will hurt you both.

How to Be Remembered

The way it starts is the way it will end. You need to realize that every time you begin a new relationship you are preparing for the way it will end. So ask yourself, "After this relationship, how do I want to be remembered?" Do you want to be remembered as a self-confident, great catch? Do you want to be remembered as the party girl? Fun? Easy? Valuable? Needy? Suffocating?

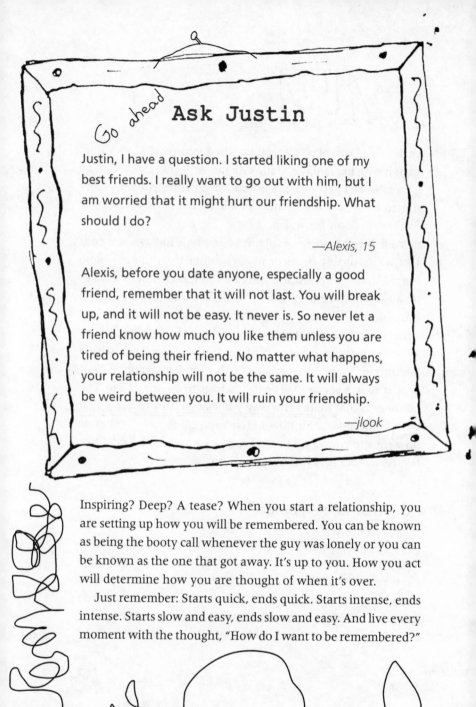

Ask Justin

Go ahead

Justin, I have a question. I started liking one of my best friends. I really want to go out with him, but I am worried that it might hurt our friendship. What should I do?

—*Alexis, 15*

Alexis, before you date anyone, especially a good friend, remember that it will not last. You will break up, and it will not be easy. It never is. So never let a friend know how much you like them unless you are tired of being their friend. No matter what happens, your relationship will not be the same. It will always be weird between you. It will ruin your friendship.

—*jlook*

Inspiring? Deep? A tease? When you start a relationship, you are setting up how you will be remembered. You can be known as being the booty call whenever the guy was lonely or you can be known as the one that got away. It's up to you. How you act will determine how you are thought of when it's over.

Just remember: Starts quick, ends quick. Starts intense, ends intense. Starts slow and easy, ends slow and easy. And live every moment with the thought, "How do I want to be remembered?"

When you do that, not only are you *Dateable,* but also your crush
will know how much he missed out on when he loses you.

Get out your journal, a sheet of paper, your e-diary, anything.
Do it right now. Don't just sit there reading. Do it. Write down this
question: "How do I want to be remembered?" Now answer it. Write
down how you want to be thought of when it ends. Like this:

> When he Thinks of me, I wanT him To
> remember me as a greaT girlfriend. I wanT him
> To Know I am precious and valuable. When iT ends,
> he will noT Know everyThing abouT me. He will
> noT have seen or experienced all ThaT I am. He
> will leave wanTing more.

Now write down how you will act to get him to feel that way:

> I am going To be mysTerious. I am going To pace
> my secreT-sharing. I am noT going To give in
> sexually. He will noT jusT come in and geT whaT
> he wanTs from me. I will proTecT myself so
> There will be so much of me he has noT seen,
> does noT Know, and has noT Touched. I am going To
> be cool, fun, and exciTing. I will Keep doing sTuff
> wiTh my friends. I will Try new Things. I will
> noT be Timid, buT I will be confidenT in who I
> am.

This is just a sample. Make it fit you. How do you want to be thought of? Once you decide, you can start playing that role. This should inspire you and excite you—you get to control your destiny. Now when the relationship begins, you can read your own future. You will be able to see that if after two years you are still just friends but getting closer, your relationship has a chance. But if you are with someone for two weeks and start talking about how much you love them, you will know that it is going to end the same way, fast and hard. When you slow down and have self-control, you are way more *Dateable*.

How to Be the One That Got Away

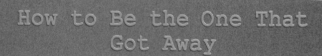

If you want to be "the one that got away," try out these things and you will drive him wild. You will be the girl he is talking about when he tells his buds, "There's just something about her. I can't get her out of my mind." You will be the treasure that got away.

1. **Be Mysterious.** Shut up and be mysterious. Go through *Girls, Shut Up and Be Mysterious*. Live it! Be a mystery that guys want to discover.
2. **Be Adventurous.** Check out *Guys, Stand Up and Be a Man*. The adventurous life applies to you too.

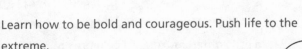

Run Granny, Run!

Learn how to be bold and courageous. Push life to the extreme.

3. *Get Involved.* Get involved in all kinds of stuff, like student council, drama, school clubs, sports, or even volunteering at a little kids program, the mayor's office, or a TV station. Get involved in apartment Bible studies, community events, or reading to people at a nursing home. Whatever it is, getting involved makes you feel incredible about yourself. Major self-esteem boost. It gives you way cool experiences that others wish they had. And it ups your social value because you have a life, you are busy, and you have interesting stories to talk about, so people think you must be cool. And here's a bonus: Guys want what they can't have. You will be so busy that you are hard to get to. You will be the thing that he can't have, he will be feeling it, and you will become the one that got away. He will say, "Man, I just gotta have her."

4. *Be Creative.* Write poetry. Paint. Sing. Cover your notebook with leaves. Shop at the thrift store. Think of new things to experience. Grab a friend and once a week do something that you have never done before. Try out new food, even if you don't think you

will like it. Go on trips. Visit museums. Live life and be a little different. You will be more noticeable when you are living life to the fullest, and you will become more *Dateable*.

5. **Be a carefree spirit.** This is a no nagging zone. Don't be a downer. Love life. Try new things. A guy wants to play. He wants to run, to experience, to push life. You will win major points if you become someone he can have fun with and someone who can be spontaneous. Don't worry about how you will look. Don't give it the bad idea stamp because your hair might get messed up. Let it get messed up. Get dirty. Forget about your fingernails and mascara and be carefree. That means "free of care" or simply "I don't care!" Stop caring about how you look or what others will think and go along for the ride. It will up your *Dateable* value.

Carefree Bonus: If you want to hit 9.8 on the Dateable Scale, initiate something fun and exciting. It could be an outdoor festival. A mud fight. A roller-coaster marathon. A spur of the moment run down the beach to jump in the ocean with all your clothes on. Do something you wouldn't normally do. Toss aside your

hairdo hang-ups and go for it. He will say, "She is just so cool."

6. *Laugh.* A smile connects people. Find humor in everything. You don't have to say it, you can just think it. Let's face it, we all do stupid stuff, so don't freak out when it happens to you. Laugh. That gets you off the hook and lets others know you don't take yourself too seriously. Don't be in a constant state of crisis. Just take it easy and stay cool.

Bonus: Laugh at him. He is going to do things a lot of times that won't be that funny. But this is part of the male ritual. We humiliate ourselves in an effort to get you to like us. Don't write us off as the mental hospital parolee; see the heart that it's coming from. Think we're cute. Please, laugh at us. That gets the guy feeling more comfortable, and he will settle down a bit. This will help us both out.

Laughter Trick: Fake it. Your body gets a buzz when you laugh. It shoots feel-good chemicals into your brain and healing chemicals into the blood to help make you healthier. And this is the cool part: Your body doesn't know the difference between fake laughing and real laughing. So fake it, if you have to, 'til it becomes real. Even if you are alone blow-drying your hair,

53

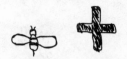

make yourself laugh out loud. Your body will jump into action and do the whole chemical thing even if nothing funny is going on. When this happens you will feel better, be happier, be more confident, and be more *Dateable*. Being able to laugh even though you sometimes don't feel like it will do great things for your health and your *Dateable* value. Laughing will get easier, and he will say, "She is so much fun to be with."

7. **Be Positive.** Let's put it like your momma taught you in kindergarten: "If you can't say anything nice, don't say anything at all!" It's true! If all you can throw into a conversation is negativity, pretty soon no one will want your opinion because they'll know it's gonna downer their happy buzz. Find positive things to say. If someone gives a negative, then you chime in with something positive. If they tell you what they don't like, you tell them something you do like. The world already has too many negative vibes going around. People want to be around others who have good stuff to say, and that includes your crush.

8. **Ask Questions.** The number one way to get people to think you are cool is to get them talking about their favorite subject . . . themselves. Ask

What?

Why?

Where is the bathroom?

questions. Ask about his interests, hobbies, life. The cool part is that in asking questions you will end up getting to talk about your interests, your hobbies, and your life.

EZ Q's: "What'd you do this weekend?" "Have you seen (name a movie)?" "How do you like our new teacher?" Asking questions isn't rocket surgery. Just ask anything. The questions will get deeper as you go. He will say, "I feel like I can tell her anything."

Do these things. Practice them. Get good at them and you will become hyper-*Dateable*.

4

4

4

4

4

4

4

4

4

4

4

If

I Will

Do It

for You,

I Will

Do It

to You

Let this ooze through your brain a little bit: If I will do it *for* you, I will do it *to* you. It's a character issue.

The Bad Side

A Liar's a Liar

Politicians argue against this point all the time. You have some guy who cheated on his wife, abused his power to make it happen, and lied to cover it up, and his supporters claimed, "This does not impact his decisions as President. His personal life is separate from his professional life." No, it's not. This is a character issue. If someone will lie to cover up a sex scandal, he will lie any time the truth could make him look bad. He's a liar. He isn't a liar in just this situation; he's a liar, period.

Same goes with friends. You might call one up and say, "Hey, I told my mom I'm spending the night with you, but I'm going to sneak out with my boyfriend all night. So when my mom calls, tell her I'm already asleep and I will call her in the morning. Okay? Bye." If your friend agrees to do it, you are both liars.

If someone will lie to your parents to keep you out of trouble, you can't believe anything they say. I know, I know. That's different, right? "She was lying to keep me out of trouble, but she's really not a liar." Yes, she is, and so are you. It's a character issue. People who lie are liars.

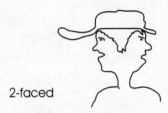

2-faced

Does this sound familiar? You have a group of friends. The four of you are really tight. But whenever one of the friends is not there, everyone else is talking about that person. ✪

"I can't believe what she wore today."

"She will never get him. He is way outta her league."

"Dude, he is so gay."

Whatever. If everyone is talking about the friend that's not in the group right at that moment, guess what they are doing to you when you're not around. Yep. Exact same thing.

"Oh, but we're best friends. They would never do that to me." Not while you're standing there, maybe, but as soon as you're not around, they will do the same thing to you. Yeah, go ahead and think about your friends right now, 'cause you know what they're doing to you when you're not around.

Blabbermouth

If you have a friend that is always "confiding" in you and telling you other people's secrets, *do not tell that person anything.* Well, don't tell them anything you don't want blabbed around, because they are going to take your news and "confide" in someone else. It has nothing to do with getting advice or needing to talk to someone. It has everything to do with the fact that they can't be trusted. If they tell you everybody else's business, they are telling everybody yours.

Blabber Blabber
Blabber Blabber

True Story

I had a best friend that I told everything to. One night my gf and I had some serious issues to deal with. I needed to talk it out, so I called my friend and spilled the story. I knew I could trust him. He listened and gave me some solid advice. The very next day, less than 24 hours later, a different friend called my gf and asked her if she was okay. I knew exactly where that came from. **My best friend was the only one who knew, and he blabbed it** "out of concern for us." It was a crappy thing to have happen to me, but at least now I know I can't trust him. I am still friends with him, but I don't tell him anything I don't want told to someone else.

Finders Keepers

One day when I was speaking at a school, someone lost a wallet with $321 in it. (Don't ask me why someone had that kind of crazy cash at school.) A student found the wallet and took it to the office with all $321 in it. Now that's character under fire—doing the right thing just because it's the right thing, not because it's a cool thing or a popular thing or even the most beneficial thing. If you have one of those friends who would have picked up the wallet, snagged the cash, and dumped the wallet, don't leave your stuff lying around, 'cause when you're not looking, he will rob you blind. If your stash comes up missing one day, go ask that friend, "Where's my money?" If they'll steal from someone else, they will steal from you. You're either a thief or you're not, just like you're a liar or you're not.

Uh-huh!

The Player = Jerk

So what does all this have to do with being *Dateable*? Lots! Girls, if you have a guy you're diggin' and he starts chatting you up on the DL until he breaks up with his girlfriend, guess what he's gonna do when *you're* his girlfriend? The exact same thing. He'll be calling some other chica, talking with her until he decides to break up with you. (If you don't believe me, see *Girls Will Lie to Themselves to Get What They Want.*) It's just his character. He will scam to get you, then he will scam to get rid of you. If he will cheat *for* you, he will cheat *on* you.

Oops!

The Loverboy

Girls, have you ever had a boyfriend tell you how much he cares for you and that he has never had anyone make him feel like you make him feel? He tells you that he wants to show you how much you mean to him and take your relationship to a deeper level—with sex, of course! (Check out *Guys Will Lie to You to Get What They Want*.) He has probably done the exact same thing to other girls, and he will definitely do it again with someone else. It's a character issue. Don't fall for it (see *Girls, You Control How Far You Go*).

Ch. 5

Ch. 8

> If I will lie for you, I will lie to you.
> If I will cheat for you, I will cheat on you.
> If I will be mad at someone for you, I will be mad at you for someone else.
> If I will do it for you, I will do it to you.

dirty rat!!

4U=2U

Why is this so important to know? What can you do about it? The more you understand why people do stuff, the more you'll be able to be in charge of your own life. Now let's look at the same line from the positive angle: If I will do it for you, I will do it to you. The good side works exactly the same.

> ## You are who you hang out with.

The Good Side

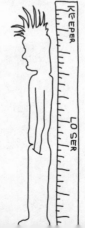

Not a Double Agent

Check it. If you have a friend who never tells you the latest juice about someone else at school and doesn't get into "asking your advice" (code word for gossip) about other people's secrets, this friend is a keeper. Her character is cool. If she will keep their secrets, she will keep your secrets.

Bodyguard ▷ Sold

If your crew is making fun of someone and one of your buds pipes up and says, "Hey, that's not cool," guess what? He will stick up for you when they are trashing you. How he treats others is how he'll treat you.

Keeper

If you try to get a friend to lie to your parents and he says, "No way," don't get ticked and ditch him with faux friend accusations. Naw, man. He's a keeper. You know that if he will not lie for you, he will not lie to you. You can trust what he says. That's good character.

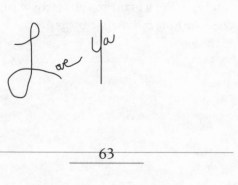

Good Catch

Girls, what if you like some guy and he won't spend major time talking to you because he has a girlfriend? When he breaks up with her and shows interest in you, he will probably be straight up enough not to cheat on you either.

Check Yourself

 You can tell how someone is going to treat you by the way he treats other people. Now flip the scope around and check yourself. You can tell your character by how you act. Will you lie? Cheat? Steal? Compromise? Are you okay with that stuff? Well, that is your character. Don't like what you see in some areas? You can change it. Change your actions and you'll change your character.

How? Here's the ADD version of how to change your character and change your life:

1. What is the **character issue** you want to change? It could be cheating, disrespecting, lying, being negative, whatever. Write it at the top of a piece of paper:
   I will stop lying and covering for my friends.

Dogpig

2. Write down all **the bad things** that will happen if you continue doing whatever it is. And make it horrible. Make it huge.

If I do not stop lying and covering for my friends, I will continue to be used by them. I won't have any true friends. My parents won't trust me, so they won't give me more freedom. I will be hanging out with friends that bring me down. I will start doing the same things that they are doing. I will stay out all night and skip school. I will be failing or making such bad grades that I won't be able to go to the school I want. I'll have to find a job. It won't be a great job because my boss won't be able to trust me. I will be stuck in a life with a low-paying job and friends that I can't trust. I will have wasted my youth and screwed up my future. I will have wasted my life, all because I continued to lie and cover for my friends.

3. Write down all **the good things** that will happen when you change. Make it great. Make it powerful.

When I stop lying and covering for my friends, my character will totally change. I will have true friends who like me for who I am and not because I will lie for them. People will know that they can trust what I say. They will come to me for advice because I will be honest with them. My parents will let me have more freedom because of my character. I will be able to get a cool job because the boss will be able to see that he can trust me. When you ask my friends and family what kind of character I have, they will say "great." I won't be worried about getting

busted for lying. I will be able to make better grades and have more fun in school because I won't be stressing over having to lie for my friends. When this happens, I will be able to get into any college I want. I will be able to graduate, get a good job, travel, and see the world. All this will happen because I stopped lying and covering for my friends.

4. To remind yourself of the change you want to make, come up with a **"trigger"**—something you normally don't do. Wear a rubber band on your wrist all the time and pop it for your trigger. Snap your fingers. Pull on your ear. Anything you normally do not do.

   My trigger is popping a rubber band against my wrist.

5. Every morning, **do your trigger** and read what you've written about your character. One good way is to pop the rubber band and read through the positive things. Pop the rubber band a couple of times while reading it too. Then read through the negative stuff. Finally, think about the high points of the positive again.

6. Do this every day for **30 days**. Then whenever you do your trigger, you will remember what you wrote. It's a good way to break bad habits and change your actions. Long-term changes in actions will change your character.

These are the basics of how to change your character. It's that simple. Let's do a run-through so we can see what it's like. Let's say your friends are always getting you to cover for them. You cover with their parents when they want to stay out all night and with their teachers when they skip class. You lie for them all the time. You want to change, but it's hard. You automatically say you'll do it because you really don't want them to get in trouble and now it's kinda expected that you will do it. But you don't want to be a liar. So let's change it.

When you do these steps, make the good seem *so* good and the bad *so* bad that you have no options. You have to stop lying. When you read these, your mind knows that changing is the only thing you can do, because if you don't, your life will be messed up. The more you read through it, the more your mind will be solid on that fact. This is called "renewing your mind."

You've also connected your trigger to the knowledge that you have to succeed. So when you pop the rubber band or do whatever your trigger is, your mind will automatically connect to, "I can't lie. I have to be honest or my life is screwed." The next time your friends want you to lie and cover for them, you will automatically want to say *okay* like normal. But pop the rubber band and all that stuff about what will happen if you do and if you don't will rush into your mind. You will remember that lying is not an option. If you lie, your life will be destroyed.

Okay, you've done your trigger, so **now what**? When your friends try to get you to provide the alibi, tell them, "No, I can't do that. Lying was messing up my life. I know that if I will

Good character and bad character can't be buds.

lie *for* you, I will lie *to* you. You can't trust me. I want you to be able to trust me."

Be ready for an argument. They will tell you all kinds of stuff to get you to do it—not because they are your friends but because they just lost their cover. For every reason they throw at you, just keep your answer simple: "No."

When you stop lying for them, they may say they are not going to be your friends anymore. Don't feel bad. Just think about what that tells you. Yeah, they weren't your friends anyway. They were just using you. But when you start changing your

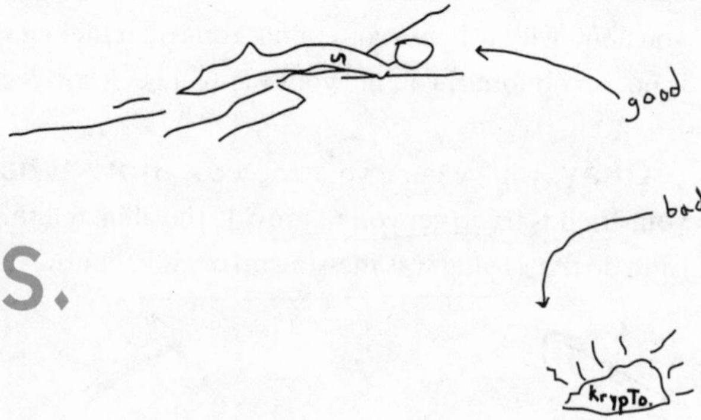

good

bad

krypTo.

character, you may have to start changing your friends anyway. See, good character and bad character can't be buds. They can hang out some, but they can't be friends. So when your character starts getting better, your friends will start getting better. You will start outgrowing old friends. Unless, of course, you have friends that are growing too. Then you get to do it together. And that is way cool.

The same thing goes for any issue: making fun of people, lying, disrespecting. When your character starts getting better, your old friends may not want to be around you. And that's great. You are moving up in the friend food chain.

Check yourself. Check your friends. Check your crush. Check your character. If I will do it for you, I will do it to you. Decide who you want to be. When you get your character nailed, you will be so much more *Dateable*.

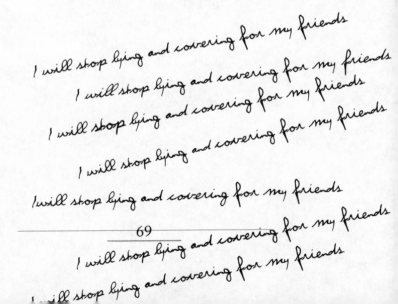

I will stop lying and covering for my friends
I will stop lying and covering for my friends
I will stop lying and covering for my friends
I will stop lying and covering for my friends
I will stop lying and covering for my friends

I will stop lying and covering for my friends
I will stop lying and covering for my friends

Guys
Will Lie
to You
to Get
What
They

Want

Guy Quiz

Frog? Or Prince Charming?

Guys, answer the following questions based on your current relationship. Give yourself a number for each word you would use: never = 0, occasionally = 1, frequently = 2, all the time = 3.

1. She has had to forgive you. ___
2. You drink. ___
3. You cheat. ___
4. You act different when you are alone together than when others are around. ___
5. She thinks she can fix you. ___
6. You borrow money from her. ___
7. She plans the dates. ___
8. You break up with each other. ___
9. You go too far sexually. ___
10. You go dutch. ___
11. You make her cry. ___
12. She does what you want over what she wants. ___
13. You treat her like one of the guys. ___
14. You fart in front of her. ___
15. You call her the wrong name. ___
16. You say she is fat. ___
17. You borrow things and forget to give them back. ___

Scoring

34-51: **Liar, liar.** *You know you lie to her, so why do you date her? Do you think God wants you lying to girls to get what you want? Check yourself, man, you're in a major danger zone. Learn to respect girls and God will honor your relationships.*

6-33: **Say no to a lie detector test.** *You ain't gonna pass. It's not cool to lie even some of the time, dude. All you have is your character. You don't wanna mess that up by manipulating women. Take it easy. Lay off on the self-obsession. Try to focus on her and her needs. It will get you much farther in the end.*

0-5: **Way to be cool.** *Your character is stellar. You are totally honoring your gf. Keep it up.*

Guys use the cheesiest lines on girls. Do you know why? Because they work! They will tell you anything and do anything to get what they want. And what do they want? Hmm . . . let me think. Guys are complicated. Deep. Multi-layered. When you get to the core of this intricate species they want . . . sex. Yep. That's pretty much it. Now I'm not saying every guy wants to throw you on the ground and get busy. But guys do want some kind of physical pay-off. And they have learned how to get it: Do the right thing, say the right thing, and you'll get a reward. It's a Pavlov's dog thing. If I'm a good boy I'll get a treat.

The weird thing is that every girl recognizes the game when it's being played on other girls. But when she is the object of these worldly arrows, it's pure romance, not devious deception.

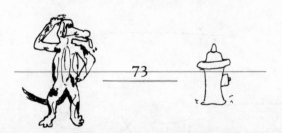

Words

Guys are thoughtful. They put time and effort into finding out what works for them and what doesn't. If what a guy says to you is believable, it's because he has practiced it. He has polished the words to perfection. Question: Where do you think he polished it? On his buds? Uh, that would be no. He fine-tuned his finesse on other girls. He played the game many times before using the exact same lines he's using on you. Yeah, I know, all that's over for him now that he found you. He was clownin' when he was with them, but he finally found you and now he means it. Right. And the tooth fairy left me a dollar last night too.

Yeah, I know, not everything is a big fat lie. But understand, girls, that it's all part of a game plan, like when you were a little kid and you had to say the magic word before you got what you wanted. Same thing with girls. A guy is trying to find the right combination of words and actions that will allow him to advance in the game.

I'm not trying to be a total downer on guys (heck, I am one). A lot of times guys don't lie, but they do use the truth to their advantage. We talked about this in *It Will Not Last:* When they tell you something, they really mean it. But they don't mean it *like that.* Like when a dude says to you, "I have never felt like this with anyone else." You believe it's because you feel the exact same way. It's like magic. You're supposed to be together. But what the guy means is that he feels *different* with you than he did with the last girl. And he will feel *different* with the next one.

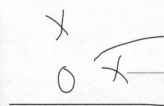

Every person is different and every person will make him feel different. So yeah, he really means it when he says you make him feel different. But he didn't mean it *like that* (see *Girls Will Lie to Themselves to Get What They Want*). It's not just a guy issue—girls are just as involved in the big lie as the guys.

This is how guys and girls are different. A guy will say, "I love you," and a girl will attach the world to it. "He loves me. He wants to be with me. We are soul mates bound by destiny. We will be together forever. I can't wait until we are married. He feels it too." Well, yeah, when the guy says it, he really means it. Seriously. He does. He loves you. And he loves his mom. He loves his car, his dog, and pizza. He loves winning the game. So when he says he loves you he really does mean it, but not the way you take it.

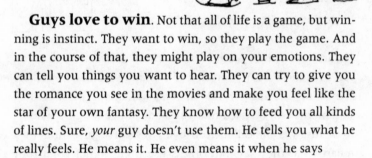

Guys love to win. Not that all of life is a game, but winning is instinct. They want to win, so they play the game. And in the course of that, they might play on your emotions. They can tell you things you want to hear. They can try to give you the romance you see in the movies and make you feel like the star of your own fantasy. They know how to feed you all kinds of lines. Sure, *your* guy doesn't use them. He tells you what he really feels. He means it. He even means it when he says

"I have never been with anyone like you before."

"I can't even make myself think about another girl."

"You are my dream come true."

"I feel like I have known you forever."

"I want to feel you close. Skin-on-skin."

"We are going to be together forever. It's like we are already married."

"You make me feel so good. I want to make you feel that good."

"I feel so close to you when we make love."

"It's not sex, baby. I want to make love with you."

"We won't go all the way, so it's okay."

"I was doubting our relationship, but now I know we were meant to be together."

"God brought us together."

"I have never told anyone else this."

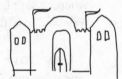

"I love you."

Girls, the reason I want you to know all this is so that you can be honest with yourself and not allow yourself to create some kind of fantasy world out of his statements. Most of these statements will be used to a guy's advantage on girls who lie to themselves and call it "true love." Yes, some guys think they mean what they say, but others use them to get what they want. So your job is to take it easy. Don't read anything into it. Don't forget, in the end, no matter how sweet he is, he is male first. And that means he has one goal, and that is the physical pay-off.

It may sound like I'm saying that all guys think about the same things whether they are spiritual or not. That's because that is *exactly* what I'm saying. "Oh, not my boyfriend. He's a good Christian guy." Yeah, and he is looking for good-Christian-guy sex. See, guys are *males* first and *Christians* second. As Christians, we let God begin to change our character. But our basic nature comes from being male. And our first thought is sex.

Actions

Guys will lie with their actions. In fact, they may use actions even more than words. You've heard that "actions speak louder than words." Well, actions *lie* more than words. The things guys do have strings attached. The best way to figure this out, girls, is to ask yourself, "Would he be doing this with his guy friends?"

I didn't come up with this. I got busted on it. I was arguing about this issue with my gf because she claimed my actions were more dishonest than my words. I said, "Prove it!" Wrong thing to say!

She asked me how many times I have rubbed my guy friends' feet. Uh . . . none!

She asked how many times I have gone shopping with my friends. "Lots!" I had her on this one. She said, "Okay, how many times have you sat around for hours waiting for them to try on every piece in the store and then walk out without buying a thing?"

Strike two.

"How many chick flicks have you gone to with your guy friends?" she asked. "None." "Okay, then why do you go to them for me?"

She made me see that I was not doing stuff for her because I was a nice guy. I was doing it for a pay-off. My own perception was way different than what she knew was reality.

A guy knows that if he sends flowers, writes letters, and gives gifts, he is working on your emotions. And he knows that this will lead to getting physical at some point in the relationship.

Now if a guy opens the door, pulls out your chair, and does all the things a gentleman does, he may be a true gentleman and not lying to you. Watch. If he does it for everyone, that is who he is. It's his character. And that's a good thing. It's not bad for a guy to act like a gentleman, and it ain't all bad for a guy to want to do girl things with you. But remember that if we weren't interested in you and looking for a pay-off, we wouldn't be doing it.

Now don't freak out completely on this, because this is normal human interaction. We all do stuff for a pay-off. I'm nice to you so you will be my friend. I don't speed so I won't get a ticket. You do your homework so your parents will be proud. I just want you to understand here that

> Guys use the emotional to get the physical. Girls use the physical to get the emotional.

hungry planet

It's Not BAD for A guy to Act Like A GentlemAn.

guys and girls often have different goals in a relationship and use different actions to get there. If you get this going in, you will be better off in the end and much more *Dateable*.

True Confessions

I hate to tell you this, but I am my own worst example. I knew this girl at school but never really paid much attention to her—that is, until all my friends started talking about how fine she was. They kept going on and on about her. Everybody wanted her. Well, I started to take notice. I still didn't really like her, but I had to have her. So I went to work.

She was on the drill team, so every time they performed, I was there. I had her "help me with my anatomy" (anatomy *homework*—get your mind out of the gutter, perv). I sent her flowers after she took a killer test. And the day I knew I had her was when I took her to a secret place for a picnic. (Of course, I had used my secret place many times, so I knew it worked.) Well BINGO, she was mine.

Yep. All mine. I still didn't really like her. I questioned myself all the time, "Why am I with her?" But I was reminded every time I was around my friends. I won! They wanted her. I got her.

The rancid thing about it all was that the girl was really into me. She believed I was doing this stuff because I really, really liked her. But it really had nothing to do with her. It was an ego trip. When it ended she was totally blindsided. I had led

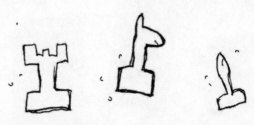

her to believe we had something special. I never said that to her because I didn't want to lie to her, but my actions said it anyway. I didn't realize that the stuff I did was lying more than my words.

Yeah, we broke up. Why do you think it ended? (Hint: See *If I Will Do It for You, I Will Do It to You*.) Yep. My friends started thinking some other girl was hot. I dropped the first one and went to the next. I fooled myself into believing that this was what I wanted to do because the new girl was special. But it was just to prove I could.

Now, does all this mean that everything guys do and say is a total scam? For the most part, no. But look at it carefully. When a guy tells you that you look nice and you do, it's not a lie. But he says it looking for a pay-off. The pay-off could be a smile. It could be making you happy. It could be making himself feel better for complimenting you. Hey, this is not all bad. It's just the way it is. Remember, guys are in it to win. This is part of the strategy. That doesn't mean he's insincere. It just means he's a guy. What he is really looking for is a pay-off.

So is there any hope for the male species? Anything worth saving? Anything worth holding on to? Yes! Teen males are on their way to becoming young men. Left on their own they will be a total waste. But they are growing. They are learning. God's workin' on them. It takes a few years of molding and pressing, but there's hope. Look at me. The stuff with the girl in my life happened a long time ago, when I was just a kid, and now I have grown and learned the value of a woman. I have learned

Time is flying

to control my actions and my words and not to use my power as a man to lie to women to get what I want. So have hope. As you mature, so will the guys around you. They won't be playing with you forever.

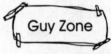

I know that it may *seem* hopeless, like guys and girls just can't get along together. But guys and girls have gotten along for eons. They have gotten married, had families, and established countries. Don't become some kind of bra-burning feminazi because all men are bad. They aren't bad, they're just different. And the truly successful woman understands that difference and acts accordingly.

If you can live knowing things aren't always like the movies, you will be closer to becoming the totally *Dateable* person you were designed to be.

Guy Zone

The secret's out. **Now what?**

Change your game from scoring physical affection to being the most powerful man. You can be more powerful than 90 percent of the male population, and it has nothing to do with benching 275 pounds or ripping phone books in half. Control your sexual desires and what you say, and you will be the guy every girl is looking for.

Hang in there, though. You'll feel like you're living that whole "turtle and rabbit" story. It will look like other guys are getting all the action and winning the race. Hang in there. Stay consistent. Control what you say. Be powerful.

Girl Zone

I've told the guys that they should control what they say and do. If you find a guy who is in control and you have watched him for a long time so you know that it's his character and not a scam, hang with him. But it's probably not going to happen anytime soon.

If you truly want to preserve yourself from being shattered, believe the truth that guys will lie to you. They will be deceitful with their words and actions. Hey, better safe than sorry. Lean toward being overly cautious about believing him. You can accept his compliments and be happy he thinks you are special, but don't think you owe him a pay-off. You'll come to lots of times when you want to believe that everything he's doing is from pure motives. But remind yourself that he's in it for a physical pay-off and an ego boost, and just accept it as that.

Girls, if you want to cherish your *Dateability,* don't get hooked by the bait that your guy throws to every girl. Hold out and hold on. Fight the urge to go with your emotions. Then you will be the prize every guy wants.

Guys, if you want to be long-term *Dateable,* chill with the lines. Don't do things to romance her and to get her to flip for you when you know it won't last. This will seem like it's slowing you down, but it's only for a couple of years. Then you will become the full-on Romeo because you will be in control. You will be the guy girls dream about. Those guys who were getting play early on? Their game will be tired and crusty. Everyone will know they are fake, and girls will be looking for the real deal. And they will want good ol' *Dateable* you.

The Exception

Some guys out there really believe they are in a relationship that *will* last. Now don't get me wrong. It's not because he is naïve and clueless. Wait . . . no, that's exactly the reason. He *is* naïve and clueless.

Bonus:

Girls, don't ask him, "What are you thinking?" This forces a guy to lie to you. He was thinking about the ball game. He was thinking about how he forgot to do his homework. Or maybe he was thinking nothing—yeah, ladies, a guy can actually be thinking about absolutely nothing. But when you ask this, he won't tell you the truth. He'll say something nice he thinks you want to hear. When you ask a guy, "What are you thinking?" you are saying, "Here's your chance. Lie to me and make me feel good."

How is that possible?

Rule of
Replacement

It's warped but true: **You gotta have one to get one.** If you have a girl, you can always get another. You simply become the perfect boyfriend to the one you've got, and it won't be long until you can upgrade to the next.

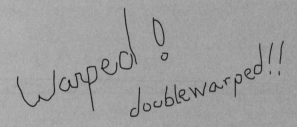

Warped! doublewarped!!

[See *Girls Will Lie to Themselves to Get What They Want* to find the semi-hidden reference to this semi-semi-random breakout/sidebar/cool orange page . . . thing . . . page.]

I spoke at a school about being *Dateable*, and afterwards a guy came up to talk to me. He was a freshman, and he was the "exception." He was sure. He told me that he and his girlfriend had been going out a while and they knew they were going to get married. They had already talked about the sexual issues and agreed to remain pure until they got married. And he let me know that he didn't lie to her either. They were honest when they told each other they loved each other. I asked him how long they had been going out. He said, "Three months." I laughed out loud. I tried not to, but I did. I said, "You're right. You are the exception. You're lying to *yourself*, not to her." It took him more than three months to learn his multiplication tables, but at 15 years old he was planning his *life* based on three months because he "just knew" it was right.

He was a great guy, just clueless. I told him to e-mail me when he breaks up with her. I said I knew he would never have to, but to keep my address just in case.

A few guys out there truly believe it will last. But beware, girls, because they may be the most dangerous kind. It's easier for them to convince you that it will last. And then it's easier for them to get you to compromise. So if you think he really, really believes it will last, be careful. He has deceived himself, and he will deceive you.

Girls
Will
Lie to
Themselves
to Get
What
They

Want

Girl Quiz

Frog? Or Prince Charming?

Girls, answer the following questions based on your current relationship. Give yourself a number for each word you would use: never = 0, occasionally = 1, frequently = 2, all the time = 3.

1. You have had to forgive him. ___
2. He gets drunk. ___
3. He cheats on you. ___
4. He acts different when you are alone than when others are around. ___
5. You think you can fix him. ___
6. He borrows money from you. ___
7. You plan the dates. ___
8. You break up with each other. ___
9. You go too far sexually. ___
10. You go dutch. ___
11. He makes you cry. ___
12. You do what he wants over what you want. ___
13. He treats you like one of the guys. ___
14. He farts in front of you. ___
15. He calls you the wrong name. ___
16. He says you are fat. ___
17. He borrows things and doesn't give them back. ___

2
1
3
2
2
3
3
3
2
~~0~~ 3
1
~~0~~ 1
1
2
1
0
2
~~24~~ 32

Scoring

34-51: *Let me just say,* **"Wake up!"** *It's time to smell the coffee. Lying is a sin, even if it's lying to yourself. And boy are you lying to yourself. If he acts like this, he's not someone you should be with. This relationship is definitely destined for failure. Get out while the getting is good.*

6-33: **You are in the danger zone**. *Looks like you are buying his lies. I know you think it isn't so bad, but if he's acting like this while he's still young, he'll only get worse as he gets older. Check it out with God. He's probably got some stuff he'd like to tell you about this guy.*

0-5: **Your lie detector seems to be up and running**. *You aren't buying any lies, so don't start now. Just because he isn't dissing you right now doesn't mean he never will. When and if he does, don't fall for it. He'll respect you for your self-confidence and your relationship will be strong.*

Now if your bf took his test (see Guys Will Lie to You to Get What They Want)*, compare scores. Don't try to read his answers, just his score. See if you are close. Do you both agree on what goes on in your relationship?*

The #1 reason girls lie to themselves is that they do not believe *it will not last*. They choose not to believe it. Girls *want* it to last. They think it *will* last. They will do anything in their power to *make* it last, even if that means lying to themselves.

It WILL last

It will last

We are different

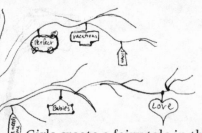

Girls create a fairy tale in their minds. As soon as you start liking a guy, you have the wedding, the honeymoon, the house where you'll live together, and names for your children all planned out. You practice writing your first name with his last name over and over. You've just met the guy or just started crushing on him, and you've created this idea of how it's going to be. Now you have to lie to yourself instead of seeing things as they really are so you can keep the dream alive.

Not only do girls auto-create this fantasia but they are encouraged to do so. Christian and general books both tell you to create *your* perfect man. So you spend hours dreaming about your true love. You can see the way he looks and the way he acts. He is strong and powerful with a passionate side. He is total romance. He knows what to say and when to say it. You have this long, detailed list of "must-haves" and "won't-tolerates." With every crush, every movie, every magazine, your list grows longer and more detailed. You do as you are taught in the "how to find romance" articles and the "I'll wait for you" books, and you fantasize about how perfect your man is going to be.

He's So Dreamy

The problem is that the next ordinary guy who comes along *is* your dream. You know it. You so desperately want to find your knight in shining armor that you believe that this guy *is* the one. He matches your list. Even if he doesn't, you convince

yourself he does. He's everything you have dreamed about. He's your soul mate.

You believe all this because you see this guy as your dream. If it doesn't work out, you refine your list, and the next guy that comes along is your perfect man. Who are you? God? You're trying to make man into your own image, the image you have in your head or have written in your journal. This is called *projecting.* You project your fantasy onto someone else, and then you believe it's true.

But in reality you have set yourself up for major disappointment. You've created your perfect mate in your mind. You've spent hours piecing together every detail. Now you've committed to wait for him. Girl, you are going to be waiting a loooong time) because what you've done is create an image that no guy can ever live up to. We are human. And worse than that, we are guys. We're going to let you down. We're going to say stupid stuff that will hurt your feelings. We're going to do things that will embarrass you. Sometimes we won't be there when you need us. We won't understand why you get so emotional. We won't be as romantic as the guy in the movie. So even though you spend your time fantasizing about your future beau, you won't find him. He doesn't exist.

I am not saying that you shouldn't have standards for who you will date. You should have standards. But make them few and basic, like these:

1. Christian: This is a must-have, <u>no compromise</u>.

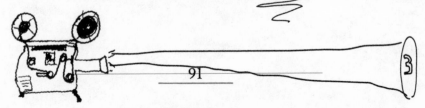

2. Non-smoker: If you can't stand smoke, don't compromise.

3. No sex: If he pushes you, he's out.

See? These are big, bold standards that you will not compromise on. Set these basic guidelines, but don't sit around concocting the perfect mate down to the microscopic detail. You will be disappointed.

Telling a girl to fantasize about her perfect guy is the same thing as telling a guy to fantasize about his perfect girl and then settle for nothing less than the perfect "10". Listen, the girl he dreams up will *not* be what the real world has to offer. She will have the perfect body. No wrinkles. No cellulite. Big in all the right places and small in all the others. She will play basketball like Michael Jordan and cook like Martha Stewart. And she will do everything he wants in the bedroom. Now he must wait until she walks right up to him without saying a word, grabs him, kisses him passionately, and says, "I'm yours!" It ain't happening. But this is the male equivalent of telling girls to fantasize about their perfect man.

Do you like me?
☐ yes ☐ no

The inner core of why girls will lie to themselves to get what they want is a hunger for acceptance. We all have it. We all want to be liked and accepted. To fulfill this need, guys will lie to girls and girls will lie to themselves.

Girls, when you are cruisin' down the road and your favorite song comes on, you start singing along, and in your romantic mind you are singing it to him. It's so obvious that the song is totally talking about the two of you. You just know he's hearing it the same way and thinking of you like you're thinking of him.

You say, "I love this song."

He says, "Yeah, me too."

You know he said that because it reminds him so much of you. Naaaa! Wrong answer. Yeah, he may tell you that, but nope, not happenin'. It's a song. We guys just listen to it. It doesn't bring up deep feelings of how much you mean to us. Girls will lie to themselves to be convinced that the song brings you together—"It's our song." But to guys, it's just a song.

The "I'm Better Than Her" Lie

Every girl knows that she is so much better than his last girlfriend. It doesn't matter what the word is about the guy. It doesn't matter what he did or why they broke up. Girls know that the real reason he broke up with those other girls is that *they* didn't know how to treat him. You know that the reason he has never settled down or stuck with a girl is that *they* didn't know how to make him happy. But *you* do! You know exactly what he needs.

You want to be the best girl he's ever had. He'll be nicer to you than he was to all the others because he really cares about

I spoke at a small school where three girls were pregnant by the same guy. Do you think they were lying to themselves?

you. Those girls were witches, and now they are just jealous. They weren't good enough. You know he chose *you* because you are better for him and more important to him.

Sorry, but no, you're not, and no, he didn't. Girls, listen to the exes. If they all say he was a jerk, they're not saying it because they're jealous. They're saying it because he's a jerk. He's going to treat you the same way he treated the others. The issue is not *your* value but *his* character.

You are valuable. You are important. But you are not more valuable and more important than the last girl. That's the same lie she told herself when she got into a relationship with him. Protect yourself. Don't think that anything you do will make him treat you better. That depends on his character.

The "I'll Fix Him" Lie

Another way girls will lie to themselves is by telling themselves that they can change him. (The older you get the more this makes sense.) "He has never changed because he has never had someone to change for. But he will want to change because of how much I love him. I will be able to make him better. He will become Prince Charming and I will be his princess." Ah yes, the battle cry of the delusional.

Yes he will!

You can't change him. It doesn't matter how much you want to or try to. He will not change for you. Oh sure, he may show progress. It may even look like he _has_ changed. But if he changed for _you,_ as soon as you break up he will go back to doing the same thing because he no longer needs to please you.

Then you'll really lie to yourself and think "Oh, he needs me" because when you're not with him he goes back to doing stupid things. That's not it. Girls, remember that he will lie to get what he wants. And he'll even lie with his actions just to please you. But he has to change because _he_ wants to change, not because _you_ want him to. So don't convince yourself that you have to be with him to make him better. If that's the case, he hasn't changed. He's just putting on a good show.

> **"He will become Prince Charming and I will be his princess." Ah yes, the battle cry of the delusional.**

The "It's Her Fault" Lie

Girls also tell themselves the "it's her fault" lie. When a guy cheats on you, you get mad at the _girl_. You're ready to rip her head off. You tell your friends that you can't wait to get ahold of her. She destroyed your relationship. She knew he had a girl-

friend, but she did it anyway. He wouldn't have done anything if she hadn't made the first move. You convince yourself that your boyfriend was just weak under the pressure. So he caved and gave into the temptation. But you'll never forgive *her!*

You know this happens. The other girl gets blamed. You're mad at your boyfriend, but instead of completely breaking up with him, you put him in relationship time-out. You don't talk to him. You don't return his phone calls. Once he has proven himself and you're convinced that he has learned his lesson, you soften up on him. He now realizes how important you are to him, and he knows he can't live without you. So you give him a second chance.

Girl, you are lying to yourself. You didn't teach him how valuable you are—you taught him that he can cheat and get away with it. You showed him that he can cheat on you, blame the other girl, and let you be mad for a little while, but you'll get back together with him once he convinces you he has learned his lesson. It's a great scam for guys. They just have to let the girl talk herself into believing her own lie. The guy gets off the hook and the other girl becomes public enemy #1. You've been played like a cheap guitar.

The "He's Just Upset" Lie

Girls will lie to themselves to excuse guys from all kinds of behavior.

and you're willing.

"He didn't mean to hurt my feelings, but he lost the game and was upset."

"He didn't mean to hit me. He was upset, and I shouldn't be nagging him when he is upset."

"The reason he drinks so much is because his home life is horrible, and drinking is the only way he can deal with it."

Girls excuse a guy's behavior as long as he has a reason. He usually wouldn't do that, but he had a reason.

Girls, this is major self-deception. *Every* action has a reason, good or bad, big or small. A guy can come up with a reason for everything he does. You believe that excuse so you can justify his actions. It's the only way to keep alive the dream that you are different than those other girls and you are the one for him.

The "Sex Is Love" Lie

One of the biggest lies that destroys girls' dreams and self-esteem is the lie that he wants to have sex with you because he loves you so much. Girls believe "It will be something so special between us." This is a total con. A guy doesn't want to have sex with you because he loves you so much. He wants to have sex with you because you're a girl and you're willing. Sure, it will be special to him. Just as special as the last girl, and just as special as the next girl . . . nothing special.

Don't read this!

Stop giving away our Secrets!!

The "We're Just Fooling Around" Lie

Some girls totally buy into the lie of "Oh, he really cares about me. He promises we won't have sex. So it's okay if we do everything else. We can do some touching, kissing, and fondling, because he won't have sex with me." Girl, wake up! You are going to do everything except intercourse until you are totally comfortable with all the other stuff. Then your sexuality will have become totally accepted and no big deal. Then guess what? You will have sex. It's just the natural progression. Stop thinking it will end up any other way. You're buying into lies that will destroy you (check out *How Much You Put In Determines How Much It Will Hurt When It Ends*). And by the way—newsflash—this just in: Oral sex *is* sex, that's why it's called oral SEX.

Ch. 2

The "Long Phone Call" Lie

Not all lies are so obvious. Some are subtle, harder to spot. But they are still lies. Like the long phone call. When a girl gets on the phone and has a great conversation with a guy, she keeps track of the time because it's a gauge of compatibility.

She gets off the phone and immediately calls her girlfriend.

The friend asks, "How'd it go?"

"We just got off the phone."

"It's been over an hour! Wow!"

"I know," she giggles. "We are made for each other because we could just sit and talk for hours."

+ SCORE

Phone Score

15 minutes or less = No Chance

30 minutes = Potential

45 minutes = Love

60+ minutes = He's the One

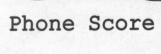

Girls, these lies are all happening on your end. On the guy's end, when he gets off the phone, he sits down on the couch and has this conversation:

"Oh, man, I missed *SmackDown Live*."

"Wow, she can talk a lot, bro!"

"Yeah, I wonder when she'll let me kiss her."

He doesn't understand the way girls keep phone score. Guys don't do it that way. He's just trying to get you to like him before you figure out he's a dork.

The "I Can Call Him" Lie

The "I can call him" lie is also subtle. You like a guy, but he isn't making a move. You convince yourself that maybe he is just shy. "He likes me, but I am going to have to make the first move. It's okay. What do I have to lose?" (The answer is "his respect," but you don't want to believe that.)

So you call him. But deep down inside, you know that's not the way it's supposed to happen. You know that you should be pursued. You should be asked. You should be the jewel being sought after. But you get in a rush. You have to lie and tell

yourself, "It's not the Stone Age any more. Girls can ask out guys." Sure you can. But don't kid yourself, the guy will get bored with you. Wait on the guy. Let him make the move. Give him the chance to be the man (check out *Girls, Shut Up and Be Mysterious*).

Ch. 13

Guy Truth: If he doesn't ask you, it's 'cuz he doesn't like you or isn't man enough to ask. Either way, he's not the guy for you.

The "He's Got Another Girl, So He Must Be Hot" Lie

What happens when a guy who has been liking you but you have totally rejected suddenly shows up at the party with a hottie at his side? All of a sudden, your feelings erupt. You notice how cute he is. How charming his personality is. He's the guy of your dreams. He is everything on your list. You have to have him! Hey, this guy hasn't changed. He's the same dude he's always been. But you have convinced yourself that he's wonderful. Why? Because someone else is with him. He *must* be great. And he must be great *with you*. It's a lie. It's kinda natural to "want what you do not have." But you don't have to act on this emotion, this lie, because when you get the guy, then what? You don't want him any more because you see why you didn't like him in the first place.

Rule
OF
Replacement

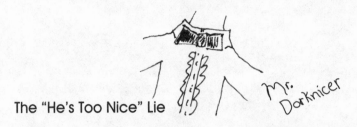

The "He's Too Nice" Lie

This lie goes to the opposite extreme. Girls tell themselves, "If he likes me, there must be something wrong with him," or "He does nice things for me. He's just too nice." Listen, there's nothing wrong with you, and there's nothing wrong with *him* for liking you. You *are* likeable. And just because a guy does nice things for you doesn't mean he's weird. It doesn't mean that he's not your type. It means he is nice and knows how to treat you with respect. Enjoy it. Savor it. Let him treat you like something special.

Don't get weirded out because you confuse honest compliments with the fact that guys will lie to get what they want. In this sitch, he's using the *truth* to his advantage. When the nice things he is saying are true, you should feel complimented and accept the flattery. Don't think that he's a jerk or a Mr. Dorknicer. All your relationships start with you and your self-confidence. When you value yourself, what others say is merely icing, not something to live or die by. When you are confident, you might know he is totally using the truth to his advantage, or you might think he is genuine—but either way you aren't manipulated by it. You just take it as a nice compliment and thank him. If you know you are worth it, you will accept a nice guy.

Easy girls
are not keepers.
They are a
temporary fix
'til the right one
comes along.

The Sum of All Lies

All of these lies boil down to one thing: acceptance. Every lie comes from the hope of acceptance and the dream that he will think about you constantly and be so into you that he can't get you off his mind. These are acceptance issues.

We all want to be accepted. That's not a bad thing. We all want to do things for others that will draw people to us. That's great. But when you start lying to yourself and doing things based on those lies, you destroy who you are. You rip apart your identity and your purpose. By believing these lies you devalue yourself and become less of a jewel to fight for.

Be truthful with yourself. Step back and see the lies that you are believing. Take control of your thoughts and actions. Look for the truth. Don't just follow your emotions. Take what they say at face value instead of trying to give it some big underlying message that he is in love with you. Most importantly, don't lie to yourself. You will be shocked at how *Dateable* you become.

The Exceptions (Guys, Read This!)

Now guys, be very aware! Yes, there are girls out there who are totally in it for the sex. They will push you. They will be all over you, fellas. These girls are the ones trying to get *you* somewhere alone. They just want the physical throw-down.

First of all, you gotta know that the only reason they do it is the way it feels—emotionally, physically, the whole deal. Prove it? Okay. If sex made you feel like someone was cutting your eyeball open and pouring salt on it, would you do it? Didn't think so. The reason *anyone* goes after sex is the way it makes them feel.

Some girls will use their sexuality to get what they want from guys. It's sad, but girls can learn early that if they show a little flesh, a dude will do anything for her. Yeah, she may be lying to herself that it's okay for her to do that, but she is playing you

Lies Girls Believe

I am different.

I am more important to him.

They didn't know how to treat him.

I love him more than they did.

I am better than his last girlfriend.

I will change him.

I am the best he's ever had.

He's thinking about me.

They weren't as nice as me.

They weren't as cute as me.

He'll be nicer to me.

He is sweeter to me than he was to the others.

I know him better than they did.

He has the power to be better because I love him so much.

It's okay for me to call him.

It's not his fault.

for a fool. Girls can use a look, a touch, a little accidental peek to drive you wild. Then they can manipulate you into doing what *they* want—because they know they can. Watch out!

Note to Girls: Your high-powered sexuality is not attractive. Yeah, it's exciting for the guy. Yeah, he will use you . . . uh, I mean, let you use him. Easy girls are not keepers. They are a temporary fix 'til the right one comes aong. You will only get a short-lived rush that will leave you alone and all used up.

Girls, once you start being honest with yourself, you will become more beautiful. Guys start really flipping over a girl who is confident, smart, and honest with herself. You will have a glow about you. An aura that attracts people. You will be more elusive and therefore more sought after. Remember, people want what is rare and hard to get.

You are a unique beauty, and once you have confidence, you will be incredibly *Dateable*.

If What You're Showing
Ain't on the Menu,

Keep
It
Covered
Up

Ever heard "Don't judge a book by its cover?" Whatever! I mean, yeah, that's the way it *should* happen. But it's not the way it *does* happen. Things and people are judged by the way they look. Looks count!

Girls, I know there are lots of things you look totally hot in. You go shopping and try on some killer threads and *wow!* It's like these clothes were made for your body. Well, duh, they were. They are totally for you. They fit in all the right places and hide all the right things. You are over-the-top sexy. You know you look good, and everyone else will know you look good too. You gotta have 'em.

During this wardrobe renovation, remember that you judge a book by its cover. Don't you? Imagine you are standing in line to ride a huge roller coaster when you notice that it looks old. It looks like it's wobbly. It looks like there are some pretty major pieces falling off. Wouldn't you think to yourself, "Hmm, Self, I don't think this is a good idea"? Yeah, you would, because we all judge things by the way they look. And that's okay.

Understand this: Guys are visual beings. They are turned on by what they see, plain and simple. Now, ladies, you find that hot little number that makes you look f-i-n-e and you bring it home. You put it on and go out in your spaghetti-strap half-shirt, flashing your stomach, with little shorts that could have been painted on. *Do not* get upset when guys just want your body. Do not call your friends and tell them what a jerk he is. Do not gripe because he could not stop staring at your breasts. Guys are visual, and they are going to stare at what you are

showing. So don't get all upset when they respond to the way you are dressed.

Girls do this all the time. You show everything you've got and then scream "all guys are jerks" when they don't care at all about your mind and just want to get with you. Well, check your fashion. You get treated the way you dress. Hey, if guys are treating you like you are EZ, you are probably dressed like you are EZ. Wait! Don't throw this book down yet. Stay with me. This is important.

Check it: I'm walking down the street wearing a policeman's uniform. I have the hat, the shoes, the badge, the whole deal. I'm walking down the street, minding my own business, when someone runs up to me shouting, "Help! I need help! I was just robbed!"

"Hey, lady, I can't help you," I say.

"What do you mean? You're an officer, you have to help."

"Oh, no. I'm not an officer. I just dress this way."

Translation: *I'm not EZ, I just dress that way.*

If this isn't enough to change your perspective, know this, girls: When you put on that little babydoll tee showing all your business, every guy from 8 to 80 is staring at you. Oh, I know, "It's fashion. That's what I look good in." That's not the point! *yeah* Your target is teenage guys. You are trying to get them to notice you. But that's not what's happening.

<u>Every man</u> is staring at you. When you wear those tight little shorts, every man is staring at your butt. When you wear the

tight, revealing shirt, every guy is looking at your breasts. Think about that the next time you get dressed. Think about your grandfather, because all of his old friends are looking at your breasts when you wear that stuff. Eww! I know it's gross, but that's the truth. If you dress like a piece of meat, you're gonna get thrown on the BBQ. It's that simple.

Yuck!

I know, when you wear super-sexy rags, you do get more attention. You feel like the guys like you more. They talk to you more. They want to spend more time with you. The truth: They don't even know who *you* are. They can't get past staring at your body. That doesn't mean they *like* you. The next chick who walks by with a hot body . . . you're history. You're easy to leave, because they never *knew* you. They just saw your bod.

If you dress like a piece of meat, you're gonna get thrown on the BBQ.

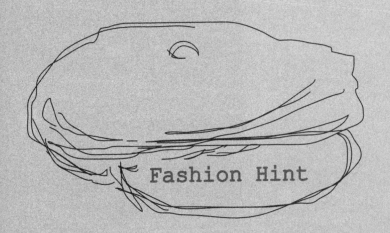

Fashion Hint

Create your own style. If you are going to rank high on the *Dateable* scale, you can't be a carbon copy of your friends.

Sure, it's okay to throw in some of the same pieces that your friends flash, but do your own thing. Be creative in your fashion. Shop at garage sales and thrift stores. **Always wear one thing that is totally out there**—a watch, an earring, a hat, anything. Just be creative and don't get caught in the fashion black hole where you look like everyone else. This will totally up your *Dateability.*

I'm not saying you have to run out and buy labels or *stop* buying labels to get noticed. But I am saying that people will treat you the way you're wrapped. If you are in a cheerleader's outfit, they will treat you like a cheerleader. If you are in a basketball uniform, they will treat you like a b-ball player. In skater gear, like a skater. You know this. What you wear will determine how you're treated.

 The trick here is to dress like you want to be treated. This goes way beyond shorts and flesh. This spills over into every aspect of your life. If you walk in to some place to get a job and you have baggy pants hanging down your rear and your hat turned sideways, talking like you do with your friends, don't get mad when the manager treats you like an irresponsible teenager. That's the way you look. It's not racial. It's not prejudice. It's not that they don't like you. It's just that they are treating you the way you are presenting yourself.

Dealing with adults is not my bag. I don't like it. But at times I have to meet with them. I like the way I normally look and dress. But I know they will freak out if I walk in with spiky white tips and wide legs. I know they'll treat me like a punk kid. So I put on what I call my "big boy suit" and go blow them away. And they treat me like the company owner I am. The hair still sticks straight up. It catches them off guard because it doesn't go with the suit, and that's the way I plan it. I totally have to dress the way I want to be treated, and they will treat me like I am dressed every time.

Just think about it. How do you want to be treated in any situation? Then dress the part. If you are going to get a job, pull up your pants, take the hardware out of your head, and leave your hat at the house. Look like you deserve the job. If you are going to the X Games, gear up and play that role. Fellas, if you are going to pick a girl up at her house, do not—DO NOT—walk in saggin' and baggin', looking like the pimp of the month. Girls, if you want a guy to respect you, dress so he can respect you.

You will be treated the way you are dressed. Remember, guys are visual creatures, so this is very important. Girls, I want you to be admired not just for your body but for *you*. I want you to be sought after. I want you to be known. So girls, dress so that you won't just be an object, but so that you will be seen as a valuable person packed in cool wrappings. That is attractive and *Dateable*.

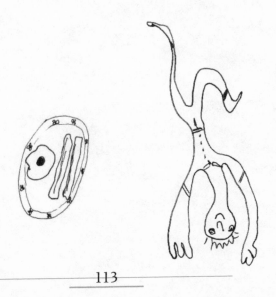

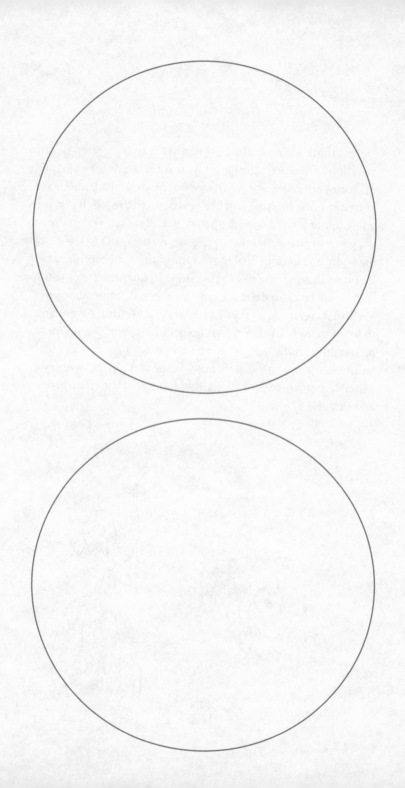

Girls,
You
ConTrol
How

    F   a   r

You Go

Ladies, let me start by saying "I'm sorry." I apologize for having to write this section. This is *not* the way it's supposed to be. The guy should be the one to stand up and say "Here are the boundaries we will not cross." That's the way God designed it. But we as men have screwed this one up.

With that, let me state the facts: Girls, you determine how far you will go. A lot of guys will push you. They will pressure you. They will lie to you and tell you they can't live without you. But you have control of what you do with your body.

Most guys think that it's the girl's job to take control of the sex area and draw the lines. Their attitude is "I will go as far as she will let me." That's wrong! But that's the way our world is. If you want more on what guys are supposed to do then read *Guys, You Control How Far You Go.*

Ch. 9

Since most guys have put it off on girls to be the man and take the lead in this area, know that you have the strength to take a stand. Remember the truth "I can do all things through Christ who strengthens me." That even means playing the role of a man if the man won't. So yeah, God has placed the strength within you.

Understand, though, that some guys will not want to take "no" for an answer. They will do everything they can to get you to cave, to compromise. They will play on your emotions. They will use

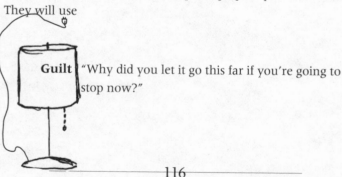

Guilt "Why did you let it go this far if you're going to stop now?"

Pressure "Come on. I just want to touch you. It's not wrong."

Love "Baby, I love you so much. I want us to be so close. Skin on skin."

All of this is manipulation at its worst. Realize what is going on. A lot of guys will tell you anything they think will work (see *Guys Will Lie to You to Get What They Want*). At some point this high-pressure guy will pressure you by playing on your emotions. When it comes to sex, assume that whatever a guy says is a lie and manipulation—unless the guy says, "I want to have sex with you. I don't care about tomorrow. I want to use you because I am really hot right now." If he says that, maybe he's being honest.

Ch. 5

Okay, have we totally pounded this issue into the ground? Guys are blamers when it comes to sexual control. They will lie to you and use you. Girls, you control how far you go. So now what?

Don't Tease the Animals

Have I mentioned that guys are visual? They get turned on by what they see (see *If What You're Showing Ain't on the Menu, Keep It Covered Up*). So listen: Please, PLEASE don't tease us. To show us your hot little body and then tell us we can't touch is being a tease. You can't look that sexy and then tell us to be on

Ch. 7

A guy will have
a tendency to treat you
like you are dressed.
If you are dressed
like a flesh buffet,
don't be surprised
when he treats you
like a piece of meat.

our best behavior. Check yourself—if you're advertising sex, you're going to get propositions.

Don't get me wrong. I'm not saying you have to be a fashion reject. I love fashion, guys' and girls'. I am all over it. But you can wear way cool stuff that doesn't show a guy all your business.

A guy will have a tendency to treat you like you are dressed. If you are dressed like a flesh buffet, don't be surprised when he treats you like a piece of meat.

Dress for your body. Get clothes that work with what you've got. But know that if you go too tight, too short, or too low-cut, you are no longer a person to get to know but an object to use.

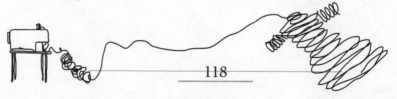

Sex Won't Keep Him

It's hard to fight this thought. It's easy to feel as if he will like you more if you go farther and farther sexually. Or, if things are going bad, that you can keep him and make it better with sex. Or maybe things are so good and it feels so right that you just know it's time. You want to show him how much you care for him. And girls, you think your fella feels the same way. He doesn't! No matter what reason you have for doing it, it's not the same for him.

To him it's sex. It won't make the relationship better. It won't make you closer. It does not show him how much you care. It's sex. Even if it's not going all the way. It's touching, it's fondling, it's sexual gratification and excitement—it's sex. It won't keep him. Sure, the relationship may last a little longer, but that's because he's *getting it* from you. It's a lot easier for him to stay than to go somewhere else and have to start over. So don't think that if you give in sexually it will win his heart. Keep yourself pure. Keep yourself safe and powerful.

Girl Power

Guys want to make you happy. They are trying to figure out what to do and say so you will like them. You have the advantage here. You have a way of controlling guys that we don't want to admit. So use this to your benefit.

Handling a sexually excited guy by telling him you want to "do something else" is more effective if you have already talked about where you stand on sexual purity.

If a guy wants to go somewhere secluded and talk or go hang out at a friend's house 'cause their parents aren't home, that's the time to use your power. Tell him you really want to do something else. And be specific, like "No, I don't want to do that. I really want to go to the mall" (or play putt-putt, or go bowling, or whatever). Say it with force and confidence. Do not say it weak and whiny, like "You know . . . uh . . . I really think I might like to do something else, like maybe go to the mall or something, if it's okay with you." No! Use your strength, feel your girl power!

If the guy doesn't agree, repeat it again. If he still doesn't, raise your voice a little and repeat it. If he *still* doesn't, tell him to take you home. Tell him you aren't feeling good, so he should take you home. It's not a lie. You really *aren't* feeling good about going to his friend's house, so you want him to take you home. It's all about your power as a woman.

And one more thing: Don't try to reason with him by telling him that because you want to stay pure, you're not comfortable

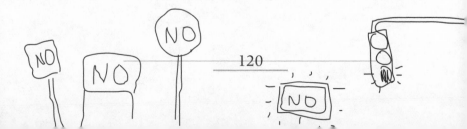

going to places where you might risk doing something you don't want to do. If you do that, you just gave him his angle—now he knows where you are coming from and how to change your mind. He'll try to convince you that nothing will happen. He'll promise that he wants to keep your purity. And suddenly you're on your way to the friend's house where you said you wouldn't go. But if you tell him you just don't want to, you don't give him anything to argue with, because he can't argue with the fact that you just don't want to go.

You should have already talked about your position on maintaining your purity long before the heat of this moment. Don't use this time to make your case. Get this book for your crush. Read through it together, especially this section and the next. The section you are about to read comes from *Guys, You Control How Far You Go*. But girls, I don't want you to rely on the guy. I'm going to lead you through the same steps I'll lead them through, but each of you should do them on your own. Do the following and make yourself more *Dateable*.

Get Symbolized

You need to know when you are going to stop *before* you get into making out and throwing clothes. Make a commitment to God. Seal the deal by getting a symbol to remind you of the deal you made with God and then with your boyfriend. Rings work great! This is a lot easier to explain as we go, so let's do a run-through so you can see how it works.

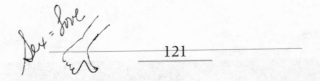

The Steps

1. Commit to the end.

Determine where you'll stop sexually. This is just YOU.
Not you and your current crush. It has nothing to do with
him. This is your deal with God. Make it very specific.
Don't just say, "We won't have sex." That doesn't work.
Try this: Think about having pictures of what you and
your bf do and having to show those pics to your mom,
dad, sis, granny, and pastor as well as his mom, pastor,
and so on. If you would be embarrassed to show and tell
. . . don't do it!

So with that, you can see that anything more than kissing
is out. Even that can be borderline, because can you
imagine showing that slide show to your granny? "Here I
am kissing his lips. Here I am kissing his neck. Here I am
with my tongue in his mouth. See, Granny, there's my
tongue right there." Yuck fest! I feel dirty just thinking
about it.

Pause. Rewind. Before you get your film developed, let's
figure out where things went wrong. It all started when
you entered the Danger Zone. In football it's called the
Red Zone. This is the place where games are won or lost.
For you it's the place where what you want to do and
what you know you should do are in conflict.

A guy's hand never "slips." He always

It's like this: Danger Zones are those places you will not go because chances are you'll end up doing things you should not be doing. They're places like in your room with the door shut. Parked somewhere alone. At a friend's house when his parents aren't home. Think of all the places that will make it easy to fall. Then decide where you will stop and what Danger Zones are out of the picture and write it down like this:

Won't Do

"Won't Do" List: Kissing is cool. But we will not get into a marathon make-out session. Tonguing, licking, and sucking is all out. Sex, oral sex, touching each other under clothes, touching each other over clothes, rubbing up against each other feeling all passionate—these are all out. He will not sit or lay on top of me. I will not sit or lay on top of him. I will not let my hands "slip," and I will not allow him to let his hands "slip." I will stop his hands when they start to roam and I will keep mine in check. We will not hang out in places that will make it easy to compromise.

2. Now focus on what you will do.

Write down what's okay, something like this:

"Will Do" List: Kiss, but not make out. Holding hands is cool. Putting my arm around him, kissing him, all good. But it stops there.

knows exactly what he is doing.

Put what you are cool with and no more. If you aren't okay with kissing, put it in the Won't Do section.

Now it's time to make the deal. Get some paper or your journal and write it out. Make it real. You might cheat on yourself, but what are you going to do, try to scam the Creator of the universe? Make it something like this:

> God, I commit to sexual purity. I know it will be hard, but I want to stay pure. My boyfriend and I will hold hands, and I will put my arm around him, even kiss him. But heavy making out and anything else is out. I commit to stopping. God, please help me. Give me strength. I make this commitment to you.

Just tell him exactly what you are thinking. Write it down so that when you have a "blonde moment" and forget what you said to God, you can go back and read the original. 'Cuz he ain't gonna forget.

If you have a hard time telling God something that you are okay with, then you are probably not okay with it. So make it something you will not do.

If you have a hard time telling God something that you are okay with, then you are probably *not* okay with it. So make it something you will not do.

3. Get a symbol.

This symbol will be a reminder of the deal you made with God. Like I said, a ring works great, 'cuz most of the time your hand is what starts exploring first. If you have a ring on when your hand starts roaming, you will either see it and stop or see it and choose to ignore it. Either way, you can't deny the fact that the ring reminded you of the deal and you have to make a choice—keep your promise with the Almighty, or trash it and dive into your passions.

If you're not the ring type, get something else. A chain, a bracelet, a pendant. Anything that you can have with you. Maybe it's a cool rock you found. Keep it with you, and whenever you are alone with your bf, put the rock in your hand on the sly. Then if your hand wants to go touching, it has to drop the rock first. You'll be reminded of your commitment.

Here's a piece of power from the apostle Paul in the book called 1 Corinthians: "No temptation has seized you except what is common to man. And God is faithful; he will not let you be tempted beyond what you can bear. But when you are tempted, he will also provide a way out so that you can stand up under it."

This is way cool. You are planning your "way out" in advance. When the ring reminds you about your commitment, that is God giving you a way out. Take it!

Do not ignore it and then ask God why he didn't help you or give you a way out. Will it be hard? Yes, at first, just like anything new is tough. But it will get easier.

What is your symbol going to be? Get it and make the commitment.

4. Let him lead.

Now we are going to give the guy the opportunity to be a man. Like I already said, get this book for your guy and go through it together. Start with *Guys, You Control How Far You Go*. You can check out this section too to get the whole scoop. But the guy should make the commitment and get his symbol on his own. Then it's time for him to take the lead. See if he will ask you to do it. If he doesn't, then one day when you are going through the book, look at his section and say, "Hey, did you do this? Can we do it together?" Please don't say, "I already did it. I'm just waiting on you to do your part." Just throw out some suggestions that you would like to do it. Remember, girls, you have already done it. You've already made your commitment to God. You know what you will and will not do. You just want both of you to be on the same page.

If your guy still won't be a man and take the lead, then show him your symbol and tell him what you have committed to. Tell him exactly what you will allow, just like you told God. Ask your guy if he will make the same commitment, not to you but to God. If he will, then go through it together. If he won't, then get out of the relationship now. He will get you to compromise and will leave you to deal with the consequences.

You have made a commitment to God. That's not something that you go back and negotiate because some guy wants to do more.

No. Returns

If your bf does agree to do this, beware, because you just might find out that he is okay with going farther than you are. That is not acceptable. You have made a commitment to God. That's not something that you go back and negotiate because some guy wants to do more. Either he makes the same commitment, or you get out. He will push you until you break your promise with God. So if he will allow more than you want, walk away, or it will turn into a stress-fest that you can't handle. But give him a chance to make the same commitment you did. Talk about it 'til you're sure he just isn't in the same place you're in.

Some guys will say okay to the commitment but not mean it. This is just another thing they can do to make you happy. They know that if they can get a foot in the door, they will have a chance to talk you out of your commitment. So don't drop your guard. He may be a good Christian guy, but he's still a guy.

5. Call for backup.

Find someone who will stick with you and help keep you straight. Make it someone you can tell stuff to and be totally honest with. A youth leader. Someone at church. A teacher you trust. Then after each date you have, tell her (and I say "her" because it can't be a guy!) about it. You don't have to go into all the details of who said what and how many times you went to the bathroom.

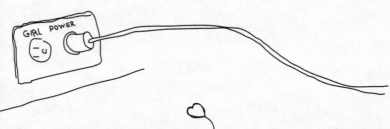

○ Did you Kiss?
○ Did you Stop?
○ Did you remember your Symbol?
○ Did he order Onions??

But tell her an overview. Give her some questions to ask you every time, like "Did you kiss? Did you stop? Did you remember your symbol?" Let her tell you if she sees any danger zones you aren't seeing. And when you push things too far, fess up to it. Let her pray for you and help you figure out how to avoid doing it again.

Girls, you control how far you will go. You are in the power position here. Guys want you. They will do whatever they can to get you to like them. And they will *not* do the things that they know will blow their chances. You are the princess. You are the reason guys fight so bravely (see *Guys, Stand Up and Be a Man*) Ch. 14 and also the reason they act so goofy. Understand this so you can use your strength. Determine how far you will go, and then use your strength to get your hottie to comply. Giving it up won't make you more valuable. Instead of making you high-designer gotta-have, it makes you dollar store leftovers. So control how far you go. Using your girl power makes you so *Dateable*.

9

Guys,
You
ConTrol
How

    F   a   r

You Go

Guy Quiz

Control Freak

Guys, are you in control, or have you given it up?
Answer each question True or False.

1. Plan a date? You never plan a date, you're the king of playing it by ear.　T　F

2. The best date is in a public place　T　F

3. The movie is out at 10:30 and her curfew is 11:30, so you go find a quiet place to talk 'til curfew.　T　F

4. Your parents aren't at home, so it's the perfect time to bring her over to watch a movie.　T　F

5. You've agreed on where you draw the line for physical stuff.　T　F

6. The only real date is one on one.　T　F

7. You push the physical as far as she will let you. She'll make sure you don't go too far.　T　F

8. If she loved you, she would go all the way.　T　F

Scoring

1. T = 2, F = 1 ___
2. T = 1, F = 2 ___
3. T = 2, F = 1 ___
4. T = 2, F = 1 ___
5. T = 1, F = 2 ___
6. T = 2, F = 1 ___
7. T = 2, F = 1 ___
8. T = 2, F = 1 ___

8–10: **You da man!** *But don't get cocky. You have to really be tough and keep hanging on to self-control. You are totally focused the right way, so keep it up. You are being a man.*

11-16: **Danger zone!** *You're close to really losing it. Don't let your hormones take over. To be a man you have to control how far you go. Right now you're way off.*

YEAH. I LOVE YOU!

Yeah, I just told the girls that they control how far you go. But that's not the way it's *supposed* to be. I had to tell them that because most guys aren't man enough to take control. Guys think it's the girl's job to stop sex. They talk a good game about being a real man, but they put sexual control off on girls. Fellas, it's time for us to stop blaming the girls by saying, "Well, she didn't stop me."

Here's the way the world works. The world says, "If you think you are 'ready,' then do it." Plus, guys have bought into

DO IT

the excuses "I'm a guy. This is the way we're supposed to be," and "I can't control it." Guys think that because they are male they are supposed to chase girls and have sex. They believe that this is what males do, and they claim to have no control over it. They claim it's natural, the way they were designed, so why fight nature? It's up to the girl to control how far they go.

That is a bunch of pop culture moon-poop. You have a choice. You can control your sexual actions. You can't? When was the last time you started crawling up on somebody in the middle of English class? See, you *do* have the power to control it. And as a guy, you are designed to be the man. So shut up with the pansy-baby whining about not being able to control it and move on.

Since the ball is in your court and you as the male have been called to take the lead, now you have to figure out how to fight the battle of sex . . . and win. Here are some wuss-free steps that will help you become the totally-in-control kinda guy that girls are looking for.

Action Plan *← wuss-free*

Plan what you're going to do when you go on a date. Plan it so you don't have time just hanging out in total seclusion. If your parents aren't home, *do not* plan to stay at your house and watch movies. Stay in view of others. You can have some great alone time in the middle of a restaurant or walking through the mall.

If the movie is over at 10:30 and she doesn't have to be home until 11:30, *do not* go park somewhere so you can "talk." You

If the movie is over at 10:30 and she doesn't have to be home until 11:30, *do not* go park somewhere so you can "talk." You may be speaking in tongues, but you won't be talking.

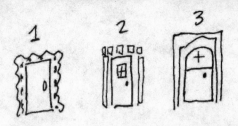

may be speaking in tongues, but you won't be talking. Go back to her house and talk there. Tell the girl why, too. Tell her that she is precious to you, you are very attracted to her, and you know that if the two of you are alone, you won't be able to control yourself. Tell her that you don't want to ruin your relationship, so you want to go where you will not be able to act stupid. Hey, if you have a good relationship with her parents, tell them. They won't weird out on you. You could tell them "Hey, I'm a guy and your daughter is beautiful. I don't want us to be in a position to mess up. So it would be great if she and I could hang out in the kitchen together. That way we get to be together, but we also know that anyone could walk in at any moment." Talk about winning points with the girl *and* getting her parentals to respect you! Hint: Don't make it a let's-sit-down-and-talk biggie discussion kinda thing. Just throw it out there like it's no big deal. Just tell them matter-of-fact-like and they will treat it like no big deal. Everyone will be cool with it.

Babe bonus: This plan-the-date thing will help you control the urge, and it also will be a big league hit in letting her know you are a take-charge kinda guy.

Get Symbolized

You need to know when you are going to stop *before* you get into making out and throwing clothes. Make a commitment to God. Seal the deal by getting a symbol to remind you of the deal

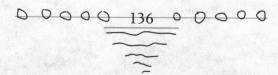

If you would be embarrassed showing your granny pics of what you're doing with your gf, don't do it!

you made with God and then with your girlfriend.

Rings work great! This is a lot easier to explain as we go, so let's do a run-through so you can see how it works.

Whoa. More steps.

Cool

The Steps

1. Commit to the end.

Determine where you'll stop sexually. This is just YOU. Not you and your current crush. It has nothing to do with her. This is your deal with God. Make it very specific. Don't just say, "We won't have sex." That doesn't work. Try this: Think about having pictures of what you and your gf do and having to show those pics to your mom, dad, sis, granny, and pastor as well as her mom, pastor, and so on. If you would be embarrassed to show and tell . . . don't do it!

So with that, you can see that anything more than kissing is out. Even that can be borderline, because can you imagine showing that slide show to your granny? "Here I am kissing her lips. Here I am kissing her neck. Here I am with my tongue in her mouth. See, Granny, there's my

tongue right there." Yuck fest! I feel so dirty just thinking about it.

Pause. Rewind. Before you get your film developed, let's figure out where things went wrong. It all started when you entered the Danger Zone. In football it's called the Red Zone. This is the place where games are won or lost. For you it's the place where what you want to do and what you know you should do are in conflict.

It's like this: Danger Zones are those places you will not go because chances are you'll end up doing things you should not be doing. They're places like in your room with the door shut. Parked somewhere alone. At a friend's house when her parents aren't home. Think of all the places that will make it easy to fall. Then decide where you will stop and what Danger Zones are out of the picture and write it down like this:

"Won't Do" List: Kissing is cool. But we will not get into a marathon make-out session. Tonguing, licking, and sucking is all out. Sex, oral sex, touching each other under clothes, touching each other over clothes, rubbing up against each other feeling all passionate—these are all out. She will not sit or lay on top of me. I will not sit or lay on top of her. I will not let my hands "slip." I will not push it by getting my hand as close as I can to see if she will stop me. I will stop her hands when they start to roam. We will not hang out in places that will make it easy to compromise.

2. Now focus on what you will do. *Will do*

Write down what's okay, something like this:

"Will Do" List: Kiss, but not make out. Holding hands is cool. Putting my arm around her, kissing her, all good. But it stops there.

Put what you are cool with and no more. If you aren't okay with kissing, put it in the Won't Do section.

Now it's time to make the deal. Get some paper or your journal and write it out. Make it real. You might cheat on yourself, but what are you going to do, try to scam the Creator of the universe? Make it something like this:

God I commit to sexual purity. I know it will be hard but I want to stay pure My girlfriend and I will hold hands. and I will put my arm around her even kiss her But heavy making out and anything else is out I commit to stopping God please help me Give me strength I make this commitment to you

139

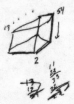

Just tell him exactly what you are thinking. Write it down so that when you have a brain cramp and forget what you said to God, you can go back and read the original. 'Cuz he ain't gonna forget.

If you have a hard time telling God something that you are okay with, then you are probably not okay with it. So make it something you will not do.

3. Get a symbol.

This symbol will be a reminder of the deal you made with God. Like I said, a ring works great, 'cause most of the time your hand is what starts exploring first. If you have a ring on when your hand starts roaming, you will either see it and stop or see it and choose to ignore it. Either way, you can't deny the fact that the ring reminded you of the deal, and you have to make a choice—keep your promise with the Almighty, or trash it and dive into your passions.

If you're not the ring type, get something else. A chain, a bracelet. Anything that you can have with you. Maybe it's a cool rock you found. Keep it with you, and whenever you are alone with your gf, put the rock in your hand on the sly. Then if your hand wants to go touching, it has to drop the rock first. You'll be reminded of your commitment.

Way Out

If you have a hard time telling God something that you are okay with, then you are probably *not* okay with it. So make it something you will not do.

Here's a piece of power from the apostle Paul in the book called 1 Corinthians: "No temptation has seized you except what is common to man. And God is faithful; He will not let you be tempted beyond what you can bear. But when you are tempted, He will also provide a way out so that you can stand up under it."

This is way cool. You are planning your "way out" in advance. When the ring reminds you about your commitment, that is God giving you a way out. Take it! Do not ignore it and then ask God why he didn't help you or give you a way out. Will it be hard? Yes, at first, just like anything new is tough. But it will get easier.

What is your symbol going to be? Get it and make the commitment.

Loser Note: You're in make-out mode with your gf, but you forgot your symbol. Don't think that's an excuse for going too far. At some point you will think, "Oh, I don't have my symbol." That is your way out. Don't be a loser. Take it.

4. Girl it up.

It's game time. Get with your girlfriend and go through this with her. The whole thing. You can even bring the book and just run through it with her. Tell her the whole story. Tell her about the deal you made. Tell her what's allowed and what's not. Remember, your deal had nothing to do with her. It's with the Creator.

Ask her if she wants to be a part of the deal. If not, back out of the relationship, because you will fall. Eventually she will wear you down or you will have an ugly breakup. Either way, you'll feel tons of pain, resentment and hate because you'll know that you could have stopped it. If she's in, then get her a symbol too. Help her find one that works for her.

You still have your commitment to God. This just gets you and your gf on the same page. Talk about what you will and will not do. Agree with your gf that when things start to get hot, you will stop. Whichever one of you gets sane enough or catches your symbol and remembers will ask the other one, "What about the deal?"

You will stop right then. No hurt feelings. No embarrassment. No guilt. Be excited. You succeeded. You fought the enemy and won. Each time it will get easier and you will get stronger and stronger.

CAUTION #1

If your gf does agree to do this, beware, because you just might find out that she is okay with going farther than you are. That is not acceptable. You have made a commitment to God. That's not something that you go back and negotiate because some girl wants to do more. Either she makes the same commitment, or you get out. She will push you until you break your promise with God. So if she will allow more than you want, walk away, or it will turn into a stress-fest that you can't handle. But give her a chance to make the same commitment you did. Talk about it 'til you're sure she just isn't in the same place you're in.

CAUTION #2

Beware of those girls who sign up but aren't really into the commitment as much as you are. Fellas, there are girls out there who are bigger horndogs than most guys. They're in it for the sex. They're into how it makes them feel. They get an emotional kick out of it. These girls are dangerous because every magazine they read tells them that if they feel ready for sex, then they should do it. They will do anything to feel like a real woman, and they think sex is okay because they feel like they're ready. They will make the commitment with you, but they are doing it to get close to you so they can get more from you. They know that if they can get you to be with them, they can wear you down and get what they want so you will make them feel like a woman. So don't drop your guard. She may seem like a good Christian girl, but she's still a human.

Beware BEAR

5. Call for backup.

Find someone who will stick with you and help keep you straight. Make it someone you can tell stuff to and be totally honest with. Your youth pastor. Someone at church. A teacher you trust. Then after each date you have, tell him (and I say "him" because it can't be a girl!) about it. You don't have to go into all the details of who said what and how many times you went to the bathroom. But tell him an overview. Give him some <u>questions to ask you</u> every time, like "Did you kiss? Did you stop? Did you remember your symbol?" Let him tell you if he sees any danger zones you aren't seeing. And when you push things too far, fess up to it. Let him pray for you and help you figure out how to avoid doing it again.

Q's 4 me!

I know, all of this sounds hard. It is. But that's the deal. You're supposed to be *the man*. You're supposed to be the leader. You're not tough and you're not a real man until you can take charge of your sexual urges. You have only two choices: <u>You control</u> *them* (or) they control *you*. If they are already controlling you, you'd better step up and start acting like a man if you want to be treated like a man. If you are in control of them, rage on. You're becoming the man you were called to be. Get ready. Girls will make you the standard of comparison to see if other guys are as *Dateable* as you.

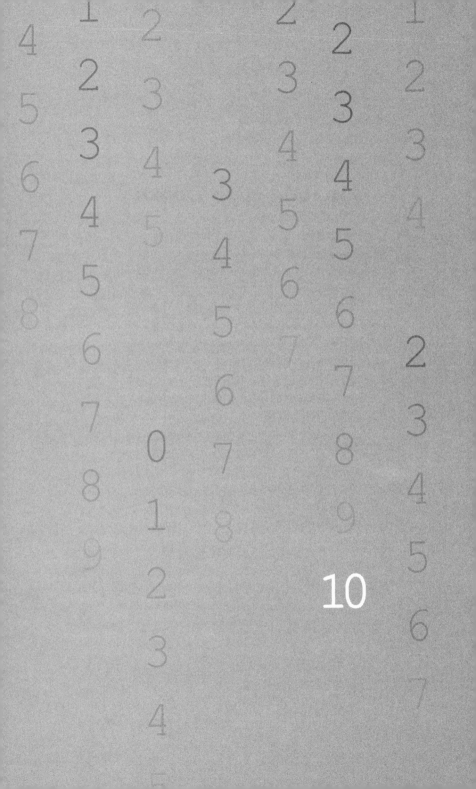

10

The Big Rub Down

Girls, isn't it so wonderful when your boyfriend
gives you a massage? You're stressed out, and it
feels so good to get the tension out. He's such a
wonderful guy, so concerned about your needs.

No, he's not! I mean, yeah, he may be a
wonderful guy, but that's not why he's massaging
you. It's a sexual thing. His hands touching you,
rubbing all over you. He's going to try to go
further and further. He's going to move his hands
lower and lower. He'll put his hands inside your
shirt so he can do a better job—well, actually, so
he can feel your bra strap and, if he's really good,
sneak a peak inside. It's sexual.

Guys, you know it's sexual. If it's not, then go
offer to massage your 93-year-old granny who

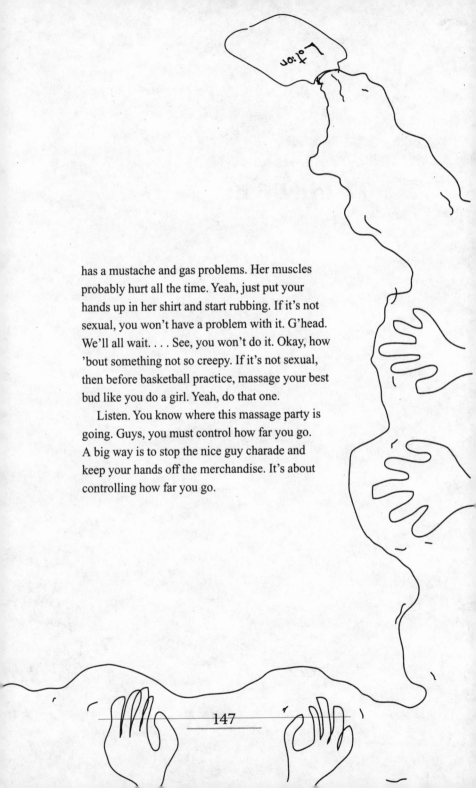

has a mustache and gas problems. Her muscles probably hurt all the time. Yeah, just put your hands up in her shirt and start rubbing. If it's not sexual, you won't have a problem with it. G'head. We'll all wait. . . . See, you won't do it. Okay, how 'bout something not so creepy. If it's not sexual, then before basketball practice, massage your best bud like you do a girl. Yeah, do that one.

Listen. You know where this massage party is going. Guys, you must control how far you go. A big way is to stop the nice guy charade and keep your hands off the merchandise. It's about controlling how far you go.

Tickle Fight

A little tickle here. A little giggle there. It's just harmless fun and flirting—or is it?

The whole tickling-flirting thing gets the juices flowing. It gets your blood pumping. Your hormones raging. A girl can see it ending like the movies. They tickle, laugh loudly, and look at each other longingly. They fall into each other's arms, kiss passionately, and spend the rest of their lives in love.

A guy also wants what he sees on the movies. They tickle, laugh loudly, and look at each other

Tickle
Tickle
Tickle
Tickle
Tickle
Tickle
Tickle
Tickle
Tickle
Tickle
Tickle
Tickle
Tickle

longingly. They fall into each other's arms, kiss passionately, and spend the next hour having sex.

Sounds crazy, but you know it's true. And for those who say I'm wrong, I dare you to come up with another reason for the tickle fight except hormone-hustlin' sexual stimulation. You can't.

This is not what I consider controlling where it's going. Well, actually, you are controlling where it's going—it's going toward sex. So the next time you have a tickle-fest, just think of it as foreplay.

Tickle
Tickle
Tickle
Tickle Tickle
Tickle Tickle
Tickle
Tickle
Tickle
Tickle
Tickle
Tickle
Tickle
Tickle

Sex Games 101:

Nap Time

Ain't it cozy? You're watching a movie with your crush. The lights are out. You're snuggled up on the couch together. You can feel his heart beating. She can feel your breath on her neck. It doesn't take the Psychic Friends Network to see where this is going.

Let's just go ahead and say this out loud (Well, you can read it out loud): *Do not get horizontal.* Yeppers. Do not lay down. Now don't ask "Well, how am I supposed to go to sleep?" I'm talking about with your crush, ya dorkasaurus.

Don't lay on the couch together. Not on the floor. Not in a store. Not on the bed. Not when you're dead. (Dr. Seuss moment, sorry!) You get

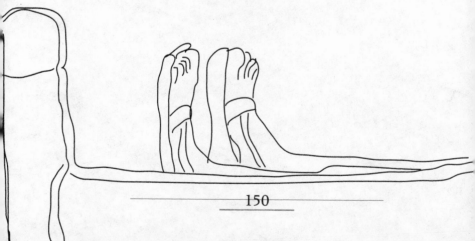

Please turn book 90 degrees to the left for the recommended bf/gf hang'n out position.

the idea. Don't take a nap together. You think it's no big deal. Hey, you aren't sleeping together. You are just, well, *sleeping* together. Totally innocent, right?

Wrong! It's not cuddling. It's not sweet. It's foreplay. You do it and you awaken the hormone giant within you. And then you spend the next two hours trying to fight off the giant. The best way to win a fight with a giant is to leave him alone and not fight him. It's easier to win the sex battle if you don't get in the position to have to fight the battle. And a horizontal position is an automatic fighting position. You may win a few skirmishes along the way, but keep doing it and you'll lose the war.

Horizontal
Bad

11111111111111111111111

Boys Will
Be Boys . . .

& you are Not one!

Girls, have you ever known that guy who's just a doll? You can talk for hours. When the two of you are alone, he is so sweet to you. He is thoughtful, quiet, respectful, even a little shy. But whenever he's with his friends, he turns into the Jerkinator! He makes fun of you. He's rude, loud, and obnoxious. He acts like you aren't even there. When he's with the guys, you try to talk with him and he just blows you off. It makes you feel like you don't belong there. The reason is . . . *you don't!*

That's right. You *don't* belong there. Hey, tell me, when a girl gets up and says, "I need to go to the ladies' room" and 12 of you form this conga line, what would happen if a dude jumped up and said "Me too" and joined the procession? That's right, you would make fun of him, think he was weird, try to get rid of him. Why? Because he doesn't belong there.

When you see a group of guys doing their thing, they are in the midst of a game. A competition. It has its own rules and its own dynamic. If you're not part of the male species, you don't get it. And if you're female and you do get it, you're going the wrong direction (see *Girls, Shut Up and Be Mysterious*).

The rules are actually pretty simple: Talk trash. Make fun of each other. Be rude. Be obnoxious. Slam each other. Those are the point-makers among the male species.

Sounds simple enough, so why can't girls play? Here's the deal: Whoever says something stupid is going to get slammed. Now girls don't speak the same language as guys, right? You know what I'm talking about. The two could say the exact same words and mean totally different things. Guys don't understand girls. They can't figure out how girls think, why

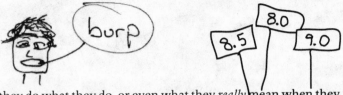

they do what they do, or even what they *really* mean when they talk. So when a girl tries to get in the guy mix, all the guys see is fresh meat! They don't understand you, so they will attack. Every guy has a new target. Even your guy. He may wait 'til you leave, but it'll happen, 'cuz if he can get them crackin' on you, maybe they'll take it easy on him. That's the way it works in the guy world.

Why? Because you're the outsider. You're the new "guy." You're easy to slam. And the more they keep the attention on you, the longer *they* won't be the target. It's all about who can be the rudest, loudest, and crudest and make everyone laugh the most. So they're going to keep pounding you, trying to get more points so they can win this round. And that's why they make fun of you.

Okay, so they'll make fun of you, but that doesn't explain the blow-off. Well, it sort of does. See, if your boyfriend is seen as too connected to *you*, then he becomes the automatic target because he is with you. Like a target by association. His immediate reaction will be to try to deflect the attention from *him* onto *you* by slammin' you. It's just part of the game. *Or* he'll blow you off so it won't look like he's whipped.

Oh yeah, that's the worst—being whipped. When a guy's friends see him doing things he wouldn't normally do or saying things he wouldn't normally say, well, it's all over for him. His friends are going to keep on and keep on 'til they find an easier target or 'til he breaks up with you. That's not the way they plan it, but that's the way it happens.

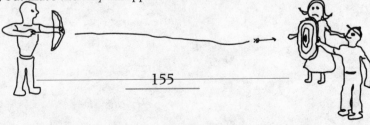

The Whip

ped Guy—

The last thing a guy wants
is to be whipped, because
that means you're controlling
him. It's like he's a big sissy
and you are his nanny, a real
ego-killer for the guy. His
friends will use this to their
advantage. It becomes ammo,
another weapon in the
game of being a guy.

Ask Justin

Justin, my boyfriend is totally different when he's with his guy friends. I don't like him when they're around. I told him about it, but he hasn't changed. I should be more important to him than they are. Help!

—*Carmella, 14*

No, Carmella, you shouldn't! Girlfriends come and go, but friends are for life. So his friends *should* be more important than you. Remember, he knows your relationship will end. On a personal note, of all the girlfriends I had in high school, I still talk to . . . um, let's see . . . ZERO of them!

—*jlook*

This is part of being a guy. It's the game we play. It's nothing personal. I know it doesn't feel that way, but guys do this to each other all the time, and they don't get upset about it because they know that's the way it's played.

I know, it's not right. Besides, you have seen the sweet side of your boyfriend, right? You wish he would just be himself. No, you don't! You really don't want a guy to be himself. What you want is to change him so that he is sweet and nice and polite. Hey, when a guy is getting loud, talking trash, burping, cutting other guys down . . . that *is* himself. That *is* who a guy is.

True

100% REAL

"Well, I just want him to be real." No, you don't! 'Cuz the real him is rude and stanky. What's fake is the way he acts with you. Wait, let me back up. It's not fake. The way he acts with you is a part of who he is, too—a very small part. But the larger part of him is the obnoxious guy, not the "sensitive male."

It sounds hopeless. With all this, how can guys and girls ever hook up? It's not hopeless. Let me give you some hints on how to deal with a guy that will make your crush less crushing.

Guy World

♥**Talk, Talk**—Never try to have a real conversation with him in front of his friends. He'll be in guy mode and you'll get slammed. You'll end up frustrated and mad.

♥♥**Sweet Talk**—Never say anything mushy in front of his friends, like "You are so sweet" or "I had a great time at the movie." Off limits. Don't do it. And never, *ever* say "I love you." When you do this, you put a bull's-eye on his forehead, and his friends are going to be ruthless. His immediate reaction will be to try to deflect the attention from him by slamming you or blowing you off. So don't do it.

♥ ♥ ♥ **Affirmative Action**—Even up the guy/girl ratio. The more you can get guys and girls together in an even way, the more everyone tries to "play nice."

♥ ♥ ♥ ♥ **Girl Friends**—Have girl friends. Have your own friends and do your own thing. Trying to be friends with all his guy friends will be a total pressure on him, and they'll get info from you that they'll use to slam him.

Some of you girls really don't get what I'm talking about. All your friends are guys. They all say you're like a little sis. You're just *one of the guys*. You're tough, you're rude, and you can hang in there and talk trash as much as they do. That's great. But you are not a girl. To them you are a guy. They'll never look at you and think "Wow, I've gotta know that girl." They'll never date you, because you're just one of the guys. Sure, you may have guys crush on you in passing, but you really won't be *Dateable* until you stop being a gal-pal.

I'm not saying that being a guy's bud is all bad. I actually think guys and girls should just hang out and be friends. I don't think you should worry about this whole dating thing until you are ready to get married. But I also know that's not reality. So

if you're going to date, I want you to be as *Dateable* as possible. And acting like a guy doesn't help your cause.

Now don't get me wrong. I'm not saying all of this to excuse guys' behavior. I'm just explaining it to you, girls. So let me say this: Guys, stop being jerks. Yeah, I just told girls what guys are like, but I never said it was good. We guys are so afraid of things we don't understand that we would rather be a butthead than appear soft.

So, guys, realize that when we do this, we're not being cool. We're being jerks. Don't do all the trash-talking with girls. It's not the way they play. Don't fart and then laugh like it's something funny. When a girl walks up, stop telling the dirty joke. It's not hypocritical, it's being a man. Some old men are just jerky little boys because they have never learned that guys are different from girls in ways other than what they learned in junior high health class (see *Guys, Stand Up and Be a Man*).

Yeah, boys will be boys. It's not always good. So guys, learn to control it. Girls, you're not a guy. Be friends, but don't be every guy's buddy. When you learn these things, you will become so *Dateable*.

Ch. 14

Good Girls
Go for
Bad Boyz

Can a Nice Guy
Get a Date?

Girl Quiz

What's Your Type?

Mark the space by the thing you prefer in your man.

___ clean cut	tattoos ___
___ Mom likes him	Mom hates him ___
___ goofy	quiet ___
___ kind	dangerous ___
___ no girlfriends	lots of girls ___
___ calls all the time	rarely calls ___
___ no piercings	piercings ___
___ opens the door for you	doesn't notice the door ___
___ gives attention	you have to work to get his attention ___
___ you know he likes you	not sure if he likes you ___
___ would never stand you up	has been known to stand you up ___
___ emotionally sound	troubled ___
___ good family	rough history ___
___ gives lots of compliments	rarely compliments you ___
___ you're his life	has his own life ___
___ sensitive	insensitive ___
___ tells you what he feels	you have to pull his feelings out of him ___
___ intelligent	artistic ___
___ open book	mysterious ___
___ never makes you mad	makes you so mad ___

___ ✿ barely touches you	kisses you passionately ☠___
___ ✿ popular	loner ☠___
___ ✿ cares if you like him	doesn't care if you like him ☠___
___ ✿ needs you	can get along without you ☠___

Add up the number of things you picked with flowers and the number of things with skulls.

More flowers. *You're into really nice guys. Don't mistake his niceness for being boring. These guys are the best catches. Your challenge is to get him to live a little, to get out and take risks. Once he starts living life with passion, you'll have your perfect man.*

hug me ;;

More skulls. *You're all about the bad boy. You love the rush. If you continue chasing bad boys, you'll go from one broken heart to the next. You'll never feel complete because he doesn't have what it takes. He's a heartache waiting to happen. Take a step back and realize that you're better than that. Live your own life and don't get caught in the bad boy craze.*

I love watching all the dating shows on TV. It's fun watching other people do stupid stuff. Have you noticed something, though? When a date isn't working out, most of the time the girl will say, "I go for more of the bad boy type."

It's true. Girls go for the bad boys. You know the ones. The guys who are untamed. Wild. Rugged. A little edgy and a little dark. Girls dig it. You see guys trying to get that image all the time. Old school Bobby Brown. Bad boy makeover Justin Timberlake.

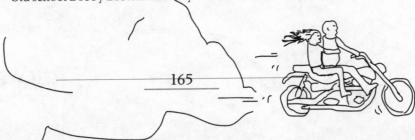

Girls, that rush the bad boy gives you is fear because you don't know what's going to happen next.

Guys are trying to pose that rebel image. Guys with a little dirt on them are more attractive. More exciting.

Here's the way it plays out in the real world. Girls like the powerful guy. The guy who's tough. Somewhat disturbed. Who knows what to say and how to "be a man." A bad boy will take a girl on a ride. He'll sneak her into bars. Kiss her passionately. Jump off bridges. The girl is on the edge of her seat the whole time. She doesn't know what's coming next. It's exciting.

Girls seek out a bad boy and hang on tight. Then they're shocked when this tough, disturbed guy turns out to be the biggest jerk. They're devastated when this dude who knows what to say and what to do starts saying it and doing it with someone else. Girls are blown away when this guy, who lives all of his life full throttle, walks out when the excitement wears off.

This happens because *bad boy = jerk*. A bad boy is exciting. So even when a bad boy starts being a jerk, it's still exciting. It's still a ride. All the girl knows is that when she's with this guy, she feels a rush. The rush is really fear because she doesn't know what's going to happen. She doesn't know if they'll have a fight, or he'll kiss her, or he'll just leave. It's exciting, but it's not healthy.

Look close at what's happening here, guys. Girls don't *really* want a bad boy. Deep down they know that *bad boy* equals *jerk*.

What they want is adventure. Girls want excitement. They want what Jesucristo described as "life to the fullest."

Why do you think the funky-mac-ugly rock stars get beautiful women? Money? Sure. But more importantly, it's that bad boy persona. They give a girl what she wants. She wants the fairy tale. She wants to be swept up in something bigger than she is. She wants a real man to take charge and give her the ride of her life.

Bad boys have been getting play because they have been the only option. Somewhere between women's lib and the modern church, guys have become pansies. We've been taught to be nice guys. Be quiet. Be timid. Don't take unnecessary risks. Don't jump without first testing the waters.

Guy Talk

Let me talk to the Christian guys for a sec. When did our Guide ever tell us to be timid, nice guys and not take risks? You'd better go back and read the history. The guys talked about in ancient Scripture were not passive. They were bold, in-your-face men. Strong. Passionate. Loyal. They were the kind of guys women want. Guys who made a choice and stuck to it. Guys who knew what they believed and were not going to back down. They were guys who dropped everything to follow their passion. Guys who would stand up for the weak. Who would jump out of boats. Fight giants. Destroy evil. They would take you on a ride that would leave you wanting more.

These were our forefathers. They were the kind of men we are called to be. Not just good little churchgoers who read the Bible and pray, but guys way over the edge. Guys making a difference in the world. Guys willing to risk without fearing the results. This is who we are supposed to be.

Listen, guys, it's time we take back our role as men. It's time to take control, be bold, and be real men. This isn't some ego kick. It's going back to our universal destiny as men. It's not becoming a bad boy. It's becoming a man that even a bad boy can't compete with. And here's how.

Man Vibe

Man Vibe 1: Passion

To be a real man, you have to live life with passion. No matter what you're doing, give it everything. Basketball. Drama. Friends. Whatever you're doing, go at it with all you've got. Even if it's just sitting around chillin', chill to the max.

Let your emotions connect with your actions. As guys, we don't understand the whole emotion thing. We would rather just act. But we miss out on the excitement of life because we refuse to *feel* life. Man, if you're sad, cry. If you're happy, laugh. Feel the emotions. Let them consume you while you take action. Don't miss out. Action is black-and-white. This is where most guys live. Emotion is the color that splashes life with excitement. Guys don't like this.

We're uncomfortable with the emotional side because we can't control it. We can't trust it. So we just live our black-and-white existence of making decisions and ignoring emotions. That's why girls think nice guys are boring. They have no color. They're nice, polite, cut-and-dry decision makers. Man, live life. Feel all that it has to offer. Be a man who makes a decision, but make it with passion.

When a girl sees a passionate guy, he's appealing. Subconsciously she knows that if you are passionate in every other area of your life, you will be passionate with her. You'll give her an experience that she can get caught up in.

Girl Note: Girls, this might be news to you. But it's making sense, isn't it? It's the way you are wired as women. Now you're starting to understand why you do what you do too.

Man Vibe 2: Confidence

Confidence is a state of mind that's often called *attitude*. The problem is that we have believed the lie that you have to *feel* confident to *act* confident. What actually happens is that when you *act* confident, you begin to *feel* confident. You don't have to *believe* it to do it, but you have to *do* it to believe it.

So how do you get confidence, even if you've never had any? Try this:

1. Soul Connection—*Eye contact*. Look people in the eye. Friends, strangers, store clerks, girls, teachers. Look them right in the eye when you talk to them. Don't stare at them like a freakazoid, just look at them. Shift your gaze from one eye to

the other. The next time you talk to your teacher, look her in the eye. It will get a little weird, but don't fold. Don't look away. Make *her* look away. Again, this isn't a staring contest, it's building confidence. The more you look people in the eye, the more comfortable you'll be with doing it and the more confident you will become.

Try this with a girl too. Girls believe that the eyes are the windows to the soul. Corny, I know, but go with it. When you're talking to a girl, no matter how nervous you are on the inside, look her in the eyes. She will feel you have connected with her through your eyes. Sounds weird, but just do it. It's respectful.

The problem is that we have believed the lie that you have to *feel* confident to *act* confident.

2. Brain Flip—Major confidence comes when you figure out that *winning and losing is not an identity, it's an event.* You lose the game, but you're not a loser. You don't wear high-dollar clothes, but you're not a loser. Your family is a bunch of weirdos, but you're not a loser. *Thank God*

Listen, you are a winner. You have things you're great at, things you can do better than anyone else. It may be computers. It may be cars. It may be making clothes. It may be writing. But you have skills no one else can do like you. Focus on those things, and figure out how to get even better at them. The better you get, the more confident you will become, and that confidence will show. You can do anything you want. You just have to decide to do it, then figure out how. Confidence is that attitude you get when you *believe* that you are awesome. It's not arrogance or cockiness. It's confidence that comes from knowing the Creator of the universe has given you specific talents that you will use. You have been designed perfectly, and you will do your part in the great plan.

3. Ego Charge—Girls like a *take-charge kind of guy.* They like a guy that they can count on to handle anything. Yeah, I know you're only one guy and can't take charge of terrorism. And girls don't expect that. They want you to take charge of *your* world. A date is a prime time to show this. You have to have a plan. Know what you're gonna do. You can let her help you decide, but you must have a plan (see *Guys, Stand Up and Be a Man*).

Take charge of your circumstances. Girls don't like blamers. You know the blamers. If you make a bad grade, it's the teacher's

That's "Ego" with ONE "G"!

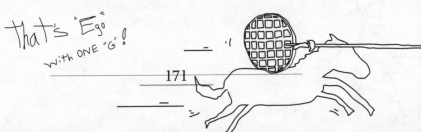

fault. If you don't get playing time, it's because the coach doesn't like you. That's not taking charge. That's being a cry baby. Instead of blaming, do something about it. If you made a bad grade . . . study. If you're not getting playing time . . . practice. This lets a girl know that when a problem comes up, you aren't going to blame others and, more importantly, you're not going to blame her. But you are going to do something about it.

Man Vibe 3: Strength

I'm not talking about lifting 500 pounds here. I'm talking about your inner strength, that force that drives *who* you are and *what* you do. Where does it come from? If you just rely on physical power, you will fail. There will always be someone bigger and badder. But it's that inner essence that makes you who you are.

What's important is that your inner strength comes from somewhere and someone more powerful than you. You've seen and heard about the samurai warriors. They would meditate on inner strength more than on physical power. And gladiators and knights were so dangerous because they knew God was worth fighting for. The Scriptures tell us about fierce warriors. David and his mighty men were some of the most feared men in their world. They were men of such force because they spent hours on their knees talking with the Source. They would not neglect time with God. Praying and studying the Word does not make you a weenie. David was known as a man after God's own heart. He would cry out to God and ask

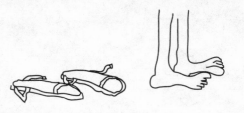

for help. He wrote many psalms of honest yelling, crying, and begging to see the Father. Because of that, he was a powerful, feared warrior.

If you're going to be a real man, you must spend time with God. He is the source of strength that will make you like the knights and gladiators. You will have the same God in you that David and his men knew. The kind of confidence and strength that only comes from something more powerful than you will pulse through your body. You will be a man of God. A man to be reckoned with. You won't back down.

Man Vibe 4: **Boldness**

Stand up for what you believe. Do what you know is right just because it's right—not because it's cool or because everyone wants you to do it, but simply because it's right.

Being bold isn't easy. That's why there aren't many people doing it. It takes guts. It takes nerve to do something when others don't agree. Yeah, every man talks a good game and they *act* all tough. But most of them are too weak to be bold when it really counts.

Like when a nerdy kid at school gets picked on by a bully while everyone just sits there. Being bold means you look the jerk right in the eye and say, "That's not cool. Nobody thinks it's funny." That's bold.

Being bold means that when everyone is talking about what they did this past weekend and you had a major God experience

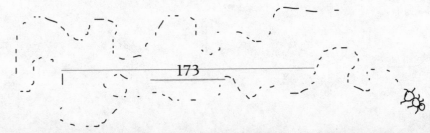

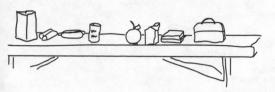

that was way cool, you tell it. You tell it with confidence. You tell it with passion. You're talking about your source of strength. You're the warrior. That's bold.

Boldness is inviting that same nerdy kid who gets picked on to sit with you at lunch. Boldness is giving your opinion when someone asks for it instead of saying, "I don't know." It's telling your friends that you don't want to hear about what they did with their gf and it's telling them why. Boldness is not backing down. It's speaking the truth. It's doing what's right, and it's way attractive.

You really wanna be bold? You really wanna step up and be a man? Go through the section *Guys, You Control How Far You Go*. Make a commitment with the Almighty. That takes nerve right there. Then get a symbol of your commitment. Take the lead and get your gf to go through it with you. Make the same deal with your gf. That's being bold. That's being a real man. That's being the kind of man that girls want to follow.

Ah

⭐ Man Vibe 5: **Adventure**

You don't have to jump out of airplanes or go white water rafting to be an adventurer (although it wouldn't hurt). You can live every day, every moment as an adventure. It's a choice.

If you don't know what it's like to live life to the fullest, go watch some little kids. To them everything is an adventure. Getting on the school bus is an adventure. Tying their shoes. Eating potato chips. Walking across the grass. Man, everything is a big deal to them.

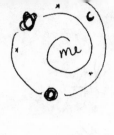

Kids have that secret talent that we forget about. It's called being impressed. Especially guys—we try so hard to not be impressed. We don't want anyone to know we are impressed, because that would mean it was something we didn't know, we didn't have, or we've never done. Guys, it's not a contest. It's not a competition. If someone scores 40 points in a game, be impressed. Don't say the other team had the worst defense in the league. If someone just went skydiving, it's okay to think it's cool. Don't try to find something wrong with it. Just let yourself be impressed. Ask questions. Be blown away. Stay away from the "that's no big deal" trap.

My grandparents live up in the Panhandle of Texas, outside of Amarillo. If you've ever been there, you know that there's nothing for miles. Then, once you get past that, there is more of nothing. I took my gf there once. I warned her ahead of time. I told her that we were going into the deepest regions of the boring and uneventful.

As soon as we got there, she was like a kid in a candy store. She wanted to see everything. We went to the Cadillac Ranch, a field with a bunch of Cadillacs buried nose-down so it looks like they are growing out of the ground. We visited the second largest cross in the world, over eleven stories high. We saw the leaning water tower. We drove along miles of fence where every fencepost had a boot stuck on the top of it. All of this stuff had become so boring to me, but this time I loved it. It felt like this was the first time I had seen it. I went from "It's alright," to "That is so cool." All because I was reminded to be impressed.

Find adventure everywhere. In everything you see and do, find one thing you are impressed with. Even if it's a restaurant or mall you've been to a hundred times, find one thing to be *wowed* by. Even in class with a teacher you can't stand, be impressed that she can talk for a full hour and be boring the entire time. That's hard to do. Be impressed. Latching onto the negatives and the don't-likes is easy. It takes effort to find cool stuff in everything. But you can do it.

Make life an adventure. Give yourself permission to be impressed. People will want to hang out with you because of your spirit. You will show them adventure in places they've never seen it. Watch what happens to your social value and your *Dateability*.

Beat the Bad Boy

Beat the bad boy profile. A girl knows this kind of guy will hurt her. He will leave her. He will toss her aside. But she has gone after the bad boy for so long, she expects to be treated

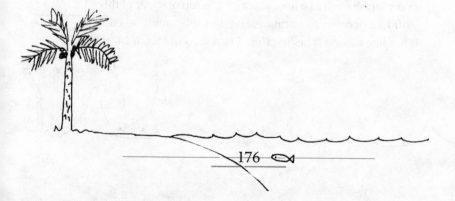

badly. When a guy is genuinely nice to her, she thinks there's something wrong with him. But you can knock the bad boy out of the preferred position by living with passion, confidence, strength, boldness, and adventure.

So to answer the question, "Can a nice guy get a date?" YES! In fact, the nice guy is the most desirable date. See, a bad boy will never get into the nice scene. It will ruin his image. This leaves him as just half a package. You, however, are the full-meal-deal. You have the nice, compassionate side that will care for her, and you have the passionate, adventurous side that keeps her excited and on the edge. You can be the best of both worlds.

Girls, I hope you can see that it's the excitement you want and not just the bad boy jerk. Fellas, I hope you see that the nice guy mixed with the adventure is what a girl longs for. You are her only hope. When you become the super-nice guy who is extremely exciting, you will be the most *Dateable* guy around.

Par-ee!

13

Girls,
and Shut Up
Be Mysterious

Girl Quiz

The Crush-O-Meter

Girls, answer each of the following true or false. When you are finished you will score your answers.

1. Honesty means telling him everything about yourself.   T   F

2. You think the faster he knows all about you, the faster he will like you.   T   F

3. You like to ask him a lot of questions.   T   F

4. It's Thursday and he's asking you out for Friday. You're free, so you say yes.   T   F

5. You had a great first date, so you call him the next day.   T   F

6. Your crush is totally shy, so you make the first move and ask him out.   T   F

7. He asks you what you're doing this weekend and you say "Nothing."   T   F

8. You are served something you are allergic to, so you talk about your health for the next 10 minutes.   T   F

9. At the end of the date there are still so many things you want him to know about you.   T   F

10. You don't respond every time he IMs you.   T   F

11. You are every guy's best friend.   T   F

Kisses

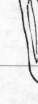

Scoring

Use this answer key and add up the numbers to your answers.

1. T = 1, F = 2	6. T = 1, F = 2
2. T = 1, F = 2	7. T = 1, F = 2
3. T = 2, F = 1	8. T = 1, F = 2
4. T = 1, F = 2	9. T = 2, F = 1
5. T = 1, F = 2	10. T = 2, F = 1
	11. T = 1, F = 2

11–14: **Dateless.** *The mystery is gone. You've probably told him everything about you, so why would he want to see you again? But it's not too late. Start talking less and listening more. Let him bring up things to talk about. Ask him questions about himself. Stop talking about yourself so much. You have plenty of time for him to get to know you. Practice thinking about him and taking your eyes off yourself.*

15–18: **Hit-and-miss mysterious.** *Cool. You've left some mystery for him to discover about you. You still might need to back off from being the one who starts things all the time, though. Let him handle the chase part of the relationship. He's a guy, let him act like one. You know what you need to do. Half of the time you do it. Try to act more mysterious more often. He'll love it.*

19–22: **Congrats!** *You're a wanted woman. You don't tell people everything in the world about yourself. You know they can't take it all in at once, so you only give them a little peek at a time. Guys are dying to find out more about you. That's what keeps 'em coming back for more. Your phone's probably ringing off the hook. Keep 'em guessing.*

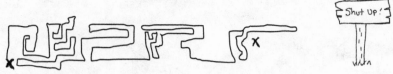

Girls, shut up and be mysterious. I know that sounds rude. But hang with me. This statement is more about guys than it is about girls.

Here's the deal. Guys love a challenge. Have you ever noticed that? Everything is either win or lose with a guy. Little girls play with dolls and get along in peaceful harmony. With guys it's "My G. I. Joe will destroy your Power Ranger!" Everything turns into a competition. "I will drive faster, jump higher, spit further, eat more, and burp louder." Guys love the battle. They love the adventure. The chase. It goes way back to the caveman days of clubbing Dino in the head for food. It's built into that Y chromosome. Hunt. Chase. Conquer. Ugh!

We're the same when it comes to girls. We want a challenge. A chase. There's just something about a girl you don't know anything about. She's mysterious. She's intriguing. A guy will do anything to pursue her and discover the unknown.

Now watch what happens, girls. You get all interested in a guy. The guy shows some interest back. He gives you a shout and you go on this marathon three-hour phone call. You love it because he is "so easy to talk to." You talk and talk and talk. You think you're really connecting and starting something new and wonderful. Then you wonder why he doesn't chat you up the next day and has moved on by the end of the week. Why? Because you told him everything. There's nothing for him to chase after. No adventure to pursue. No uncharted territory to explore. No challenge. You dished it all out and there's nothing left.

Even a

fool

is thought

wise

if he

keeps

s i l e n t .

—Book of Proverbs

Girl World/Guyville

Girls do things because it feels right. It feels natural to you, so you think the guy feels the same way. Well, he doesn't. And this goes way beyond phone convos. Check it out, here's a translation chart for girls—what you think and what guys think about the same sitch.

Girl World

Marathon Phone Call

This is so important to me. I give compatibility ratings based on how long we spend on the phone and how much share-time was involved.

Me Asking a Guy Out

I think it's okay to ask a guy out. Hey, if you want it, go get it. I don't have time to wait for you to ask. I need to know if you like me. Besides, it's cool to call guys. It's a high-speed world and it takes a high-speed girl to get what she wants.

Guyville

Marathon Phone Call

When you give me all the hidden info, there's nothing left to chase. And even though I might act like I want you to talk more, I don't. I will just get totally overloaded and lose interest fast.

Girl Asking Me Out

Sure, it's an ego kick when you call me. It feels kinda cool. But after a while the excitement wears off. There's no chase involved. You're just too easy, so I lose interest pretty soon. But the cool side is that I would rather let *you* take the risk of being rejected than me. That way I don't have to stand up and be a man—I can let you do it.

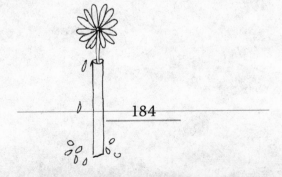

Telling My Secrets

This is a super-deep connect for me. It means a lot to mesh with you emotionally. The more I can play show-n-tell, the more I feel connected.

Hearing Your Secrets

Slow down. I'm not ready to deal with all your secrets and life traumas. I just want to have fun and adventure. Sure, I'll listen and even feel for you, but if you load me down too much I'll need some space. Keep it cool on all the gory details. At least only give me a few at a time. Save the rest for your girlfriends.

Note: *For a guy this gives a connection that he can't deal with and isn't ready for—or he just doesn't care. And remember, girls, this relationship will end. When it does, you're stuck with someone who knows your deepest secrets and has no loyalty to you. So your business will become everyone's business.*

Peep it, chicks. The things you do to feel that connection with a guy are actually making you your own worst enemy. It's like stuffing your bra. Sure you see quick results, but they don't last. And once the secret is exposed, you are totally humiliated.

Let's make something clear right now. What I am saying is *hold back*. Don't just spill all your personal info to the guy. What I am *not* saying is you need to be some little quiet girl who never says *anything*. No way. Have a personality. Laugh, chat, be as crazy and fun as you want to be. Being mysterious doesn't mean being a wallflower. It means you release your inner self slowly. Pick and choose what you say. Give the guy something to hunt for. A challenge. Make yourself an adventure for him to seek. And keep the phone convos short. Make him hang up and say "Dang, I can't wait to talk to her again," not "Dang, that girl can talk!"

Embrace your feminine mystery and become *Dateable!*

HOLD BACK

The Big Mess-Up

Guys want to play the relationship game, and they want to win. The problem is that girls have made the game too easy. It's like offering him a game of Chutes and Ladders when he wants maximum overload *Survivor*. Sure, you're trying to be helpful, take charge of your life, and get the guy you want. But you're blowing your advantage. You're destroying your chance to attract the guy of your dreams by committing the big mess-ups: Girls Pursue It, Girls Plan It, Girls Cover It, and Girls Pay Off. They are the unwritten vibe of relationships. These are all guy issues (see *Guys, Stand Up and Be a Man*), but girls have to face them too. Read 'em and learn.

Mess-Up 1: Girls Pursue It

This is the #1 thing destroying the balance of guy/girl existence: Girls have decided to pursue guys. They have started calling guys. Asking them out. Pursuing them at school. Chasing them. This totally goes against guys' nature. Sure, we are flattered and will respond. We like it. It's an ego boost. And we may even get into a relationship with a girl who pursues us. But we know it won't last because we aren't doing anything. There's no challenge. No mystery. Ever heard a guy say, "She's smothering me"? Translation: "She's chasing me, and I'm bored with it."

Ever heard a guy say, "She's smothering me"? T r a n s l a t i o n : "She's *chasing* me, and I'm bored with it."

So, girls, sit back and let the guy come after you. A guy needs to pursue. Let him be the aggressor and make him want to fight to know the deepest you. He'll love it! And he'll keep coming back for more.

Mess-Up 2: **Girls Plan It**

One of the best ways to tell if a guy is really into you is to see what kind of effort he puts into dating you. The problem comes when girls take it on themselves to plan it all out. Sure, you're good at it, but that's not the issue. A guy will work hard for something he wants. So let him take control. Give him suggestions for what you would like, or if you want to do something cool in town, tell him. But let him take the ball and do what it takes to make it happen. If you get together every weekend just

1.) pick restaurant ☺
2.) make reservations
3.) buy flowers ❀

A guy will spend money on something he thinks is valuable.

to hang out or go to the movies, he's really not interested in you. But you'll never know if you don't let him take the lead.

Don't accept excuses if he never plans anything, either. It's not an age thing, a money thing, or a time thing. If he isn't willing to plan something for you, he isn't really interested in you.

Mess-Up 3: Girls Cover It

Yeah, we're living in the new millennium. Yeah, girls have the same kind of cash power as guys, if not more. Yeah, sometimes it's good to pay for your own stuff. But a guy will spend money on something he thinks is valuable.

I'm not saying that he needs to blow crazy cash trying to impress you. If he doesn't have a big roll to blow, that's fine. You can suggest to him that you do something that doesn't cost a lot of coin. Lots of cool things don't cost much, if anything. Check out the weekly events in the paper. Find something new

and fun to experience. But the guy has to step it up and reach in his pocket.

Girls, if you are paying all the time, the guy will start feeling really weird. Most guys will start feeling like less of a man, maybe without even knowing why. So what you thought you were doing to *help* the relationship will be the thing that drives him to someone else.

So, girls, your job is to suggest new, fun, free or low-rent things you can do together, and his job is to plan the details. Remember, it's not the cash value but spending the time together that's important.

By the way, if the guy *isn't* feeling weird when you are paying for stuff, watch out! He might just be looking for his own little sugar mama.

Mess-Up 4: Girls Pay Off

Now I'm not *just* talking about a back seat, throw-down, givin' it up kind of thing. What I *am* talking about is any physical payoff. It could be holding hands. It could be a hug. A kiss. Guys are looking for anything that will feed their egos and satisfy their desire for the physical. And girls often give it freely.

Girls, giving your affection to a guy right away doesn't make you more valuable. It doesn't make him like you more. You just give him a prize without making him fight for it. He didn't have to pursue you. He didn't have to make an effort and plan. He didn't invest *any* money. And now you give him a prize—a kiss,

a hug, whatever. That totally trashes its value. It's like giving a first place trophy to a guy in the bleachers at a soccer game. He didn't have to practice. He didn't have to invest any time or money. No battle. No fight. Nothing. But he gets the trophy anyway—a trophy that's worthless to him because he didn't have to win it or earn it.

It's the same with your affection if a guy doesn't invest the time and energy to get you. You become worthless, worth *less* than you would have been had he done the work. You become *just another girl*. Sure, he'll enjoy you for the moment. But you're nothing special. Nothing valuable. He didn't earn the right to be with you.

Do you see it? Do you catch how things are supposed to flow? Guys want to put the effort into you. We want you to be a challenge. Yes, if given the chance we *will* take the lazy way out. We will let you do everything. But that's not what attracts us. That's not what keeps us coming back for more. We have to pursue. We have to plan, to pay. We've gotta have the challenge. If you want a guy to know how valuable you are, you have to *act* like you are valuable.

I know your next question is "What if I'm mysterious and don't pursue a guy but he never makes the move?" Glad you asked. Let's check the dude's issue. There are two possible answers:

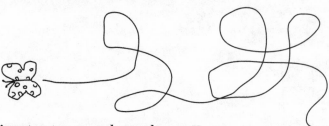

1. **He's not gutsy enough to ask you.** He expects you to make a move and take the risk. That tells you a lot about his character: He won't stand up for you. He won't protect you, your thoughts, or your feelings. He wants what's easy. As soon as you hit a bump in the relationship, he'll ditch you and move on. This kind of guy also wants a sure thing. When *you* approach the guy, it lets him know that you are a sure thing. Repeat. It lets him know that *you are a sure thing!* Even if you're not, he thinks you're an easy target.

2. You have to face the fact that **he's just not interested.**

Girls, listen, *you are valuable.* You *are* a person to be honored. You *are* desirable. You *are* worth the effort to do whatever it takes to win your affection. Guys *want* to fight for you. It's the desire of their hearts to rescue the beauty.

Here are some *Mystery-Enhancing Tips* for you that will drive guys wild.

How to Attract a Guy with Little or No Effort

Tip #1—Keep parts of your life to yourself. Don't tell him every single thing. Keep the mystery alive.

But wait! There's More!!

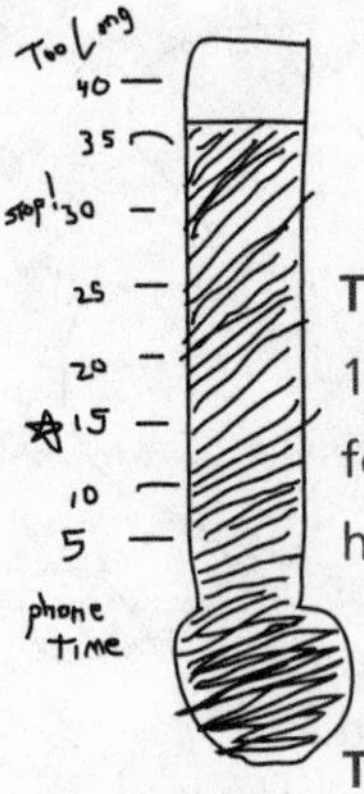

Handwritten thermometer labels (left side): Too long, 40, 35, stop, 30, 25, 20, 15, 10, 5, phone time

Handwritten near clock: ring, ring, ring

Tip #2—Limit phone calls to 30 minutes MAX. Actually 15 minutes is even better, but that will take a miracle for most girls. This will limit your talk time and leave him wanting more.

Tip #3—Always have something else to do so you have to get off the phone. Set a timer. Let the guy know that you have to go because you have plans— and always *have* plans! It can be anything. You don't have to tell the guy what your plans are. You may just *plan* to sit and watch TV. You may *plan* to go to the mall. You may *plan* to stop talking to him. Just say, "Well, I gotta run. It was great talking with you." This will totally increase your mystery factor.

Tip #4—Never accept a quickie date. If it's Friday and a guy says "Hey, would you like to go to the movie on Saturday?" tell him, "Oh, I wish you would have asked me sooner. I have plans." If you accept, you will be seen as the go-to girl for when he doesn't have anything better to do.

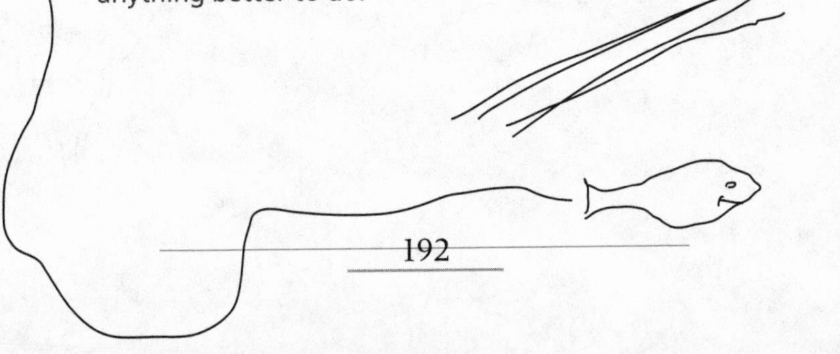

When you practice these *Mystery-Enhancing Tips,* two things will happen. First, you will protect the mystery, and this will cause the guy to want to find out more, so he'll *have* to pursue you more. Second, it will up your social value. When you have something else to do besides sit on the phone and chat all night, you become a person whose time is valuable. When you can't go on the last-minute invite, a guy will try to figure out how to get on your calendar. You will become much more *Dateable.*

I hope you see now that when I say *shut up and be mysterious* I mean nothing but love and concern for you. I want you to be confident. I want you to be the powerful woman you were made to be. I want you to be super-attractive and mega-*Dateable.*

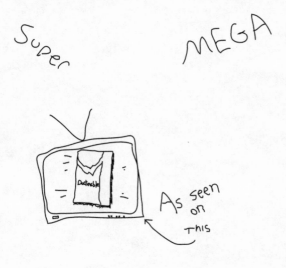

14

Guys,
Stand Up and
Be a Man

ALready

Guys, this whole women's lib thing has less to do with *women* getting rights and more to do with *men* becoming pansies. This isn't a discussion about rights. It's about what the Creator of man did. How he set things up. It's about the roles of males and females. How we are wired and why we are that way.

John Eldredge wrote a book called *Wild at Heart,* a must-read for every guy and for every girl who has a guy in her life. I love what he says:

> Society at large can't make up its mind about men. Having spent the last thirty years redefining masculinity into something more sensitive, safe, manageable and, well, feminine, it now berates men for not being men. . . . "Where are all the *real* men?" is regular fare for talk shows and new books. *You asked them to be women,* I want to say. The result is gender confusion never experienced at such a wide level in the history of the world. How can a man know he is one when his highest aim is minding his manners? . . . Now let me ask my male readers: In all your boyhood dreams growing up, did you ever dream of becoming a Nice Guy? (Ladies, was the Prince of your dreams dashing . . . or merely nice?)

Yeah! I get totally amped every time I read that. It's about guys standing up and taking on our role as men. Fierce, powerful, protective, passionate men.

Ch. 12 First go check out *Good Girls Go for Bad Boyz.* Get that stuff in your brain. Then we can really look at what being a man means in your dating life. Next check out the mess-ups I talk about in *Girls, Shut Up and Be Mysterious.* Girls are messing things up because gender-confused *guys* have forced *girls* into becoming the men. Guys have let the girls take control while they just sit back like a fat man after a tub of Ben and Jerry's. That's not the way it was designed.

Man Rules

① Guys Pursue It, ② Guys Plan It, ③ Guys Cover It, and ④ Guys Back Off—these are the baseline for all relationships. They are the roles and duties we have been given as men. Here's the way it should be in the context of girl/guy relationships. Let's break it down.

Man Rule 1: **Guys Pursue It**

Our total failure at rule #1 was the beginning of the wussing down of guys. And we have done it to ourselves under this high-and-mighty thought of equal rights and freedom. We sit back and wait for girls to ask us out. It's fair. Girls should have the same freedom as guys, right? Wrong! Well, right, but this is not a freedom. It's a responsibility. Guys are okay with girls asking them out not because we're interested in girls having the same freedom but because we don't want to take the responsibility.

Guys like it when girls ask them out. Oh yeah, it's great. The #1 reason guys say they like it is because it takes the pressure off. Yeah, it does. It takes the pressure off the guy and puts it on

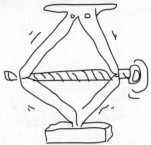

the girl. The same amount of pressure is still there, we just don't have to deal with it. No wonder guys are so okay with it.

Anytime someone asks another person out, they're taking a big chance. It means putting yourself out there and risking rejection. Our male egos don't like being rejected, especially by a girl. This is why guys like it when girls ask them out—because they can reject the girl and not have to take the risk. It's the biggest weenie-pose a guy can take. We can be in control. We don't have to worry about getting shot down. We have the choice. We can blow her off, and there's no stress on our side.

Fellas, be a man. Hey, if you're too scared to ask her, then you're not man enough to go out with her. But listen, being scared is not a bad thing. It's normal. We *all* get scared when it comes to asking a girl out. So dive in. You asked for adventure, this is it. Don't expect *her* to call *you*. Don't expect *her* to ask *you* out. Do something. Be the man. Take a chance. Ask.

Ch. 13 I've already let the girls know that they should not be doing it (see *Girls, Shut Up and Be Mysterious*). They'd better not call you. They'd better not chase or pursue you. Hey, if you have a bunch of girls always asking you out and you never step up to the plate and do the asking, that doesn't show how big a stud you are. It shows how big a wuss you are. It tells everyone that you're not man enough to pursue a girl. You're so scared that you're not going to step up to the challenge. You're acting like a wimp. Take the lead. You have it in you. Let her know you're a real man.

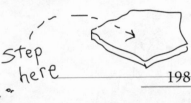

step here

or here

This is hard to try to change sometimes, because a girl coming after you is a major ego boost. But guys, be man enough to admit that once the ego thing is over, you will get really bored really fast. Hey, no chase, no challenge. No challenge, no reason to stay with her.

If you're too scared to ask her, then you're not man enough to go out with her.

"Butch"

Big Wuss!

Pansy

Man Rule 2: Guys Plan It

The Plan

When you play a ball game, you have a plan. Something to go by. You don't have to know exactly what's going to happen pass-by-pass, point-by-point. But you have a general idea, a game plan. Well, when you go on a date, have a plan. It doesn't have to be a minute-by-minute schedule of events, but you need a general idea of what's going to happen.

The Re-Group

Now once you *have* a plan, you'll have to be ready and willing to alter it. Don't be so hardheaded and unwilling to go with the flow that you lose your date. If you wanted to go to a ball game but she has a megaheadache and the crowd would be a killer, be ready and willing to move on to something else.

The Scouting

Do some advance work, too. If you're going to a new movie on opening night, get tickets in advance so it won't be sold out. Try ordering online if you can't get to the box office. If you're trying out a new restaurant, call and make reservations a few days before. If you're going to a museum or zoo, find out the hours to make sure it's open. A little advance planning will save you a lot of embarrassment and let her know you care enough to plan ahead.

Guys, you know that if something is important to you, you will invest a lot of time in it. Part of asking means you have a plan. It does *not* mean you connect with your girlfriend and go through the insanity of

"Whadda you wanna do?"
"I don't know. Whadda you wanna do?"
"I don't care. Whatever you wanna do."
"I don't care. You decide."
"No, you decide."

Somebody decide already! And it should be the guy. If you ask a girl out, you'd better plan the date.

The Rico Way

Here's a Rico Suave way to be a man and keep her in the decision loop:

> "Hey, I thought we would go grab a bite at Zeek's Hamburgers, then hit the seven o'clock show. How does that sound?"

First, this lets her know that you thought enough to have a plan. And second, it lets her have some input just in case she hates Zeek's.

Man Rule 3: Guys Cover It

Fellas, when you ask a girl out, be ready to pay. Don't be mooching off her all the time. Hey, if you're like most of us, you don't have a fat roll of unlimited cash. That's cool. Plan something that doesn't cost big bank.

You gotta pay to play. It's not a male ego thing. That's what expecting a girl to ask you out is. This is just . . . well, a no-brainer. This isn't about you gotta have money to get a girl. It's about being a man.

Look. What if your coach invited you to go out on the town. You played an awesome game, and he just wants to say congrats. He has picked this really cool place to eat and then he's going to take you to a virtual reality arcade. You are totally amped. You go eat, and man, you chow down. You even get dessert, and it is gooood. The check comes out and coach says, "Your part is $23.50."

Wait, that's not right. He invited *you*. He's taking *you* out. *He's* supposed to pay. *Exactly!* If you ask a girl out, be man enough to pay. I'm sure you're saying, "But wait a minute, by the time

we go to the movie and get popcorn and stuff, that's almost 25 bucks. I don't have that kind of cash." Well, then don't ask her to a movie. Ask her to do something you can afford. That's part of the deal.

Again, if something is worth a lot to you, you'll save up and invest your cash in it. Same with a girl. If she's worth asking out, she's worth doing something that *you* pay for.

Man Rule 4: Guys Back Off

Hand check!

Guys, give up the pursuit of a physical favor and back off. I'm not just talking about a rompin', rubbin' sexcapade here. I'm talking about any physical gesture, any pay-off. It could be holding hands. A hug. A kiss. Whatever. But guys, it is not your right to take it. In fact, it's not your right to expect this as a pay-off for the date, the money you spend, or the cuteness of your face. Your job as a real man is to guard her body. That means even from yourself.

See, it's all about the game, fellas. If you play to win, you gotta play the whole game. You have to pursue, plan, and pay in order to get the prize. You know it's true. If some girl just gives it up and hands you a kiss or a hug or even more, you know you're going to win quick and walk quick.

When a girl seems to be all into you, yeah, you're stoked when she starts making moves. You're excited that she wants to get physical. That's why it's so hard to stop it. But guys, we

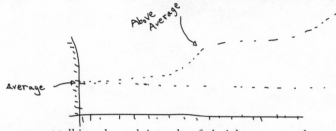

are not talking about doing what *feels* right or even what comes naturally. It's about *stand up and be a man!*

This is a calling to be more than average. It's a challenge, a dare to rise to what you're supposed to be—a real man. Take control of the situation. Don't just go with the flow because that's what she wants. You're the guardian of the princess, not the wimp who goes with the sexual flow.

Listen, guys, in the game of "love" (and that's what it is for girls, "love") girls will often give as much as you push them to. It may even seem like that's what they're into. But most of the time it isn't what they really want. What they want is for you to love them and for the two of you to connect. (Note: There are some girls who really only want sex—stay away from them.)

If you tell your girlfriend that if she gives too much too quick then you will get bored and walk away, I guarantee she will stop. Tell her that you love the challenge and a fast win means a fast game-over, and she will change what she does. She thinks the fast pace will win your heart. But once she understands that a fast pay-off is a speedy deal-breaker, she will do what she can to help make the relationship better. Bonus for you and her.

So, guys, you are not doing her a favor by leading her in the physical direction. You are not doing what she *wants*. What she *wants* is a relationship that will last. But take the physical affection too quick and you are doing the thing that will destroy it.

Be a man. Take control. You control the pace of the relationship. Do the best thing for you, for her, and for the relationship. Slow down and don't take the physical for free.

How to Be the Man Girls Dream Of

1. Sex Ready. You should already have handled this in *Guys, You Control How Far You Go.* You made a commitment to God. So don't think you can break it and get away with it. You won't. Also, understand that girls don't *owe* you anything. Not a touch, not a hug, not a kiss. So don't force any issue. Let the girl feel safe with you. You won't look like less of a man. To her, you will be even more *Dateable*.

2. Risky Business. If you really want to up your image, try this: *Do* something. It doesn't matter what. Just get involved somewhere. If you can take a trip to study in a foreign country, go. Play basketball. Join the debate team. Volunteer at a radio station, a TV station, a nursing home, the mayor's office. Anywhere. Cool people are people who have stuff going on, not guys who go to school, come home, and play video games. Get a life.

Take risks. Every week do one thing that you have never done before. Big or small, it doesn't matter.

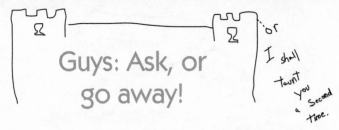

Guys: Ask, or go away!

...or I shall taunt you a second time.

Make this part of who you are, part of what you do. Then when you have a girlfriend, take that into your relationship. Together, experience one new thing per week. It could be eating somewhere you've never been or riding the biggest roller coaster in the world. Just make sure you do it.

Remember, girls want adventure. They want excitement. So ask yourself, "If I were a girl, would I go out with me?"

3. Pop the Q. Guys, you start crushing on some girl. You talk to her all the time. You ask her friends about her. (Like you think they won't tell her what you asked.) You e-mail and call her. You do little things for her. You know you like her. She knows you like her. Everyone knows you like her. Well, I'll say it just like a girl told me: "Ask, or go away!"

That's right. Kick out of sissy mode. Quit acting like your granny driving down the interstate. Pick a lane and drive in it. If you want to date her, ask. If you don't, walk away. But don't just keep acting like you really like her and not risk anything.

A final thought: A girl should always be better off because she has been with you. You have a responsibility to take care of the girl—spiritually, emotionally, and physically. When the relationship ends, your gf should be better off than when it started. She should be stronger spiritually because of your commitment to God. She should be stronger emotionally because you were sensitive to her dreams and passions. And she should be better off physically because you honored her body and didn't try to take it. Guys, we need to ask ourselves before we do anything, "Will she be better off for this?"

We are the leaders. We are the pursuers. Be an adventurer. Be a warrior. Be a gentleman. Be the package. You will be what females desire. You will be their knight. Their excitement. Their love. You will stand out above the rest and be the ultimate male . . . totally *Dateable*.

Cool Man Quote

It is not the critic who counts, not the man who points out how the strong man stumbles, or where the doer of deeds could have done them better. The credit belongs to the man in the arena, whose face is marred by dust and sweat and blood, who strives valiantly . . . who knows the great enthusiasms, the great devotions; who spends himself in a worthy cause; who at the best knows in the end the triumph of high achievement, and who at the worst, if he fails, at least fails while daring greatly, so that his place shall never be with those cold and timid souls who knew neither victory nor defeat.

—*Theodore Roosevelt*

Teddy

"Historical Dude"

' Cool dude '

$ 15 $

If
You
Wanna
Play,
You
Gotta
Pay

The Truth about Getting What You Want

Here's the deal behind the deal. You want a relationship? You want all the stuff you see on TV and the movies—the hot bod, the great hair, the steamy sex life, the romance, the whole deal? You want all the excitement and pleasure of a relationship? Okay, then are you ready for the responsibility and investment that it takes to *have* a relationship? It's the battle of getting what you want versus paying the price. Let's play connect the dots. Let's hook up the *want* with the *cost* of getting what you want.

1. **You wanna have a gf or a bf?**

Then here's the cost. Be ready to put that person first. Even before yourself. You are not only responsible for keeping yourself happy, but you also have to keep the other person happy. You have to learn what *they* like and don't like. You have to know what makes *them* happy or sad. You have to put *them* ahead of everything. You have to be ready to be there when they're rude, mean, or sick as well as when they're nice and fun. You have to be ready to drop all the other hotties. No chatting up anyone else. It's just you and your crush. That's what it takes to keep the relationship rolling. It's not all about *you* any more. It's about them and you.

2. **You wanna have sex?**

Get ready to pay the price. Be prepared for everything that goes along with sex. Guys, you'd better be ready to drop

Can I
can I
can I

210

out of high school, get a job, and support your girl and the baby when she gets pregnant. Girls, I have two words for you: "morning sickness." Be ready to be fat and sick for 9 months and to be judged by everyone else 'cause you got knocked up. You'd both better be willing to live in a low-rent apartment, not buying new clothes or CDs because you gotta buy food and diapers. You'd better be ready to get married. Sex is a big deal. Sex is a marriage game. Be ready to lose your social life. Be ready to get insurance, a doctor, furniture. You'd better be willing to be a parent and teach your child how to be a man or a woman.

Something else you'd better be ready for: In a few years, after having sex with each of your gfs/bfs, when you finally find *the one* you want to marry, know how you are going to tell them you have herpes. Be ready to go to the doctor and get the prescription you'll have to take to

Average Salary by Education Level

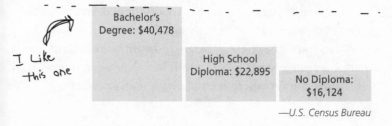

Bachelor's Degree: $40,478

High School Diploma: $22,895

No Diploma: $16,124

I Like this one

—*U.S. Census Bureau*

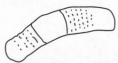

help control the outbreaks. Be ready for the love of your life to walk away from you because they know that if you get married you will give them herpes. Be ready for that. It's the chance you take.

You have to be prepared for what could happen when you start having sex.

3. Guys, you wanna ask a girl on a date?

Be ready to do what it takes. Be ready to plan it out. Be ready to know how you're going to meet up. Know how she's going to get home safely—walking or riding the subway home alone is not an option for her. Be ready to pay for everything you plan. Be ready to take "no" for an answer. Be ready for her to not want to go out with you again. Be ready for her to want a deep relationship, which takes us back to "You want a gf?" Be ready to talk with her. Be ready to open the door, to be polite, to put her before you. Be ready to make her feel special and not expect anything in return.

4. You wanna test drive the car?

But what's the cost of the test drive?

I've heard it so many times from both guys and girls: "You don't buy a car without test-driving it first." It sounds like a solid reason for having sex. I mean, you want to know if you are compatible sexually before you lock yourself into that exclusive, forever-type relationship, right? But not everything

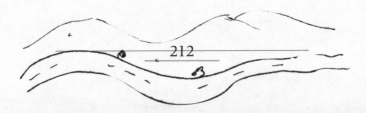

that sounds logical makes good sense when you really think about it. Let's break the logic down and see what's really being said. It's not as black-and-white as people think it is.

The Comparison Chart

Holding hands	Looking at the car. Running your hands over the hood.
Kissing	Sitting in the seat. Grabbing the steering wheel.
Heavy making out	Starting the car. Turning all the dials. Wiping your feet on the carpet. Spilling a drink in the seat.
Touching, kissing, fondling, groping, anything except intercourse	Scratching the paint. Breaking the window. Poking holes in the seat.
Sex (oral, intercourse, anything else)	Driving the car like crazy. Putting on major miles. Driving at high speeds. Running over curbs. Totally ragging out the car.

Question? Would you buy a beat-up, old, used car at a new car price? Think about it. Would you look at a car that's all scratched up with dents and high miles on it, pay the full sticker price, and think, "Wow, what a great deal"? No way. But that's exactly what happens when you get into sex without being married. When you keep having sex and pushing for a bigger and bigger

sexual high, what you are actually doing is turning yourself into a used car. Then you expect someone to come along and make a full-price commitment for a ragged-out, used car.

Every new sexual experience when you are not married puts another ding, another scratch, another scar on who you are. You keep running your car into other people, and then you wonder why no one treats you special. You can't understand why no one wants to make a major commitment.

You are in control of this. You control what kind of condition you are in. If you treat you body like an old clunker, don't be surprised when everyone wants to take you for a spin and then go get a new car. You are valuable. Keep yourself new. Keep yourself unused. Then you will be the one everyone wants, and they will be willing to make the long-term commitment to have you. You will be desirable and *Dateable*.

☐ AIDS
☐ HERPES
☐ Syphilis
☐ OTHER

Dang, that's huge. Check it. At whatever point you are not willing to do everything it takes or not ready to accept the possible consequences, stop. If you want a gf or bf, but you aren't willing to do all the stuff that goes along with it, then for Gunta's sake, do not get one. You don't have to have one. Don't get a gf/bf until you're ready for the responsibility.

If you're just out trying to get some action but you're not ready for all the responsibility, keep your pants on. If you're not ready to be a 16-year-old mommy or daddy and a high school drop-out who has to work to support your kid for the next 18 years, if you're not ready for herpes, AIDS, or any other diseases

. . . don't have sex. It's that easy. You start having sex and you're saying you're ready for all of that. Kids. Herpes. Drop-out. Just bring it on.

A man passes his biggest test in life when he can say he's not ready yet. You will show strength and wisdom by saying "I'm not ready for sex. I'm not ready for all that comes with it, so I'm not ready for it." The most powerful men in the world are the ones who have control of themselves and their sex drive. If *it* has control of *you*, you lose. But take control and your power and passion for life will multiply. Sex will be great when you're ready for one woman for life.

And girls, your biggest test is passed when you can control your emotions and see beyond your imagination. You show amazing grace and beauty when you won't sell out your body for love. You become a woman of mystery when you don't allow your emotions to lie to you about something you don't have. The power of a woman is in her ability to manage her emotions and not let her emotions control *her*.

Your challenge is this: Guys, you must control your physical body, and girls, you must control your emotional body. Do this and you will be totally *Dateable*.

The Porn Biz

Female Porn

Female pornography. This is the #1 thing that distorts a girl's view of reality, men, and relationships. Maybe you haven't heard it called female porn. Maybe you know it by the softer, more acceptable terms of "chick flicks" and romance novels. Yep. Female porn equals chick flick. These movies (and romance novels) are directed straight at women. It gets you excited, which draws you into the story and keeps you coming back for more.

Your porn isn't sexual, it's romantic. But it gives you a warped view of men. Suddenly you think all men should be sexy, romantic, dangerous, daring, beautiful, etc. The perfect man never has to go to the bathroom, never has gas, and never fights with his love or bugs her. In a two-hour sitting this perfect man saves the world, romances the girl, and takes her on the ride of a lifetime. You watch this and fantasize about your hero. You become aroused by what you see and hear on the screen. You desire it. You dream about it. You are emotionally and sexually turned on by this fictitious man.

This stuff turns you on so much because it takes advantage of that God-given desire that John Eldredge talks about in *Wild at Heart*—your inborn desire to be rescued and revealed as beautiful. For two hours you soar with the feelings of being saved by your knight in shining armor, and it arouses your feminine passion, your dreams and your hopes. And suddenly you long for the man on screen.

Then you are released into the world of real men with real flaws who cannot satisfy the desire in you that was ignited by female porn. If you have a man in your life, you begin to look at him in light of Mr. Perfect, and he can't compare. He'll never be as beautiful or romantic as the movie star with all the makeup and good lighting. See how it mimics male porn? It creates men who rescue you from out-of-control buses and shower you with rooms full of roses. They fly you off to Paris for the weekend and save you from the evil villain bent on destroying the world. *These men don't exist.* Consciously or subconsciously, you are doing the same thing men do to women by dreaming of that supermodel—you are imposing an impossible set of demands on your guy.

If you don't have a man, you begin to feel depressed because you are so alone. The worst thing you can do if you feel horrible about being alone is to go watch a chick flick or read a romance novel. This female porn takes your focus off your true purpose and passion and places it on your insecurities and misdirected passion. You'll get a man in good time, and all the daydreaming in the world won't make him come along any faster. It will only make your solitude more miserable.

So be careful, ladies. Don't be fooled. Female porn is every bit as destructive as male porn. Protect your mind. Protect your heart. If you want to stop feeling miserable when you compare your life to the ones you watch and read about, then stop watching and reading female porn. Refocus your energy and your mind. Where you put your thoughts, your heart's gonna follow.

Male Porn

Guys, just imagine a world where the women have the hottest bodies and the most beautiful faces, and they all want *you*. They will do anything as long as they get to be with you. They have to have you.

Yeah, baby! Sign me up. It seems so perfect. You get to experience all these women with no negatives. They don't get mad at you and they won't cramp your style. They're not upset with you because you didn't call. They give you total acceptance and willingness. You are a stud! The ultimate male.

Beep! Beep! Quit hitting snooze and wake up! It's time to get out of bed and stop dreaming. Close the magazine, get off line. Let's analyze this fantasy of yours to see what's really going on. It seems like this porn stuff is just between you and the computer screen, or you and the magazine, or even you and the scrambled cable channels. But it's not. It's so much bigger than that. And it isn't harmless or healthy.

The fastest-growing destructive force in man's relationship with women is the distorted image of women created by pornography. Guys fantasize about these ultimate women. They detach from reality and place themselves in the images they see. It's *you* having sex with the beauty. It's *you* being begged for more. The girls are perfect. They have perfect bodies and are willing. They become objects to be used for your own satisfaction and then left until you are ready for more.

But I've got news for you: This fantasy isn't helping your sex life at all. In fact, it's ruining it. Porn desensitizes you sexually. It makes you less sensual and sexually aware. It numbs you. Rather than enhancing sexual pleasure, it takes it away and replaces that pleasure with guilt. Then it adds a strain on your relationships. You start to hide your stuff. You lock yourself in your room hoping no one will find you. You become a one-man pleasure machine that doesn't really need anyone to satisfy you sexually. And there you sit, alone and lonely, with only one-dimensional women to keep you company.

But let's say you venture out into the world of "real women" and hook up with a girl. Major letdown. She ain't gonna measure up to your 1-D cutie. She isn't going to be airbrushed to perfection. She isn't going to be a hot little nympho bent on satisfying your sexual fantasies. She is going to be human, fragile, gentle, rough, and vulnerable, and you aren't going to know what to do with her. In the end you'll end up alone in your room with your fake women who can't even talk to you. Porn doesn't make you a sex machine—it makes you a sex dumpster.

17

Dateability

Dateable—having an internal sense of confidence, control, and sexuality that inadvertently attracts members of the opposite sex, resulting in positive effects before, during, and after the relationship.

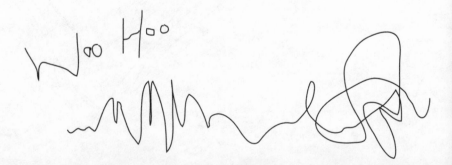

Blue sky . . . .
nothing but blue sky . . . .

This has not been a philosophy book or a "what if" book. It has simply been the truth. It's like saying the sky is blue—that's the truth. Now it's up to you to decide *what it means to you*.

But please don't run off and become a hermit. You *are Dateable*. But also know that you don't *have* to date. The great thing about being *Dateable* is the power you have when you realize you don't *have* to date. It's the same way the power of a strong man comes when he refuses to beat someone up even though he knows it would be easy. Enjoy the feeling. Enjoy the rush.

I know that some of you will stop dating because that's what this book said to you. Others will get out of the house, gain some confidence, and become a social butterfly because that's what this book said to *you*. Everyone gets something different, something that was meant for them. The things that I hope you *all* got are that you are *Dateable*. You *can be* the one everyone wants. God cares more about who you are than about who you date. You were made for success and for a purpose. You were made to complete your destiny. Pour yourself into that, and the dates and the *Dateability* will come naturally.